GW00570322

THE SINGING-MASTERS

THE SINGING-MASTERS

John O'Meara

LILLIPUT PRESS
DUBLIN

First published in 1990 by
THE   LILLIPUT   PRESS   LTD
4 Rosemount Terrace, Arbour Hill,
Dublin 7, Ireland

A CIP record for this
title is available from
The British Library.

ISBN 0 946640 68 8

Jacket design by The Graphiconies (Ramaioli)
Set in 12 on 14 Van Dijck by
Koinonia Ltd of Manchester
and printed in England by
Billings & Sons Ltd of Worcester

For my wife Odile and our children
Dominique, Catriona and Odile

[Your letters] will speak to me of
Christ, of Plato, and of Plotinus.
– Augustine, *Letters* VI.1.1.

O sages standing in God's holy fire
As in the gold mosaic of a wall,
Come from the holy fire, perne in a gyre,
And be the singing-masters of my soul.
– W. B. Yeats, 'Sailing to Byzantium'

PROLOGUE

THIS IS not only some account of my earlier life: it is also some account of the formation of my mind and its preoccupation, from early consciousness, with ideas that can be described as Platonic and Christian. The method of the book is not that of prolonged analysis of a psyche: the matter is approached through action, through the recounting of episodes and anecdotes that are frequently far from solemn. Did not even Socrates address himself to serious matters with light-heartedness, and a touch of irony? Wordsworth's 'Ode on Intimations of Immortality from Recollections of Early Childhood' supplies a text for each of the chapters.

ONE

Heaven lies about us in our infancy!

MY FIRST shadowy recollection is of my father pausing at the
end of my brass and iron cot at night to look at me. The
recollection must indeed be shadowy, since he died on the 29th
of December 1915, when I was just over ten months old.
Doubtless this is a projection of something told later to me by
my mother, who had a tendency to rehearse the past and the
capacity to make one relive it with awed attention. My earliest
firm recollection, however, is of my 'realization' that I was
encompassed by an insubstantial world. What I saw before me
– people, houses, trees – was but an image which disappeared
when I turned around, to be replaced by a new image at my
back. The 'world' fell away immediately behind and immediately beneath me. It was a frightening thought, but fortunately
I was not always occupied in thinking. What was uppermost in
my mind, however, when I did think, was the knowledge that
I was on trial and was usually found wanting. This was
discouraging. All the beings around me, principally my mother,
my aunt, and my younger brother Patrick, the maid, and the
yard-man, were agents of some Great Being who manipulated
all. They too, however consistent and continuous, were images
that appeared and disappeared. I was alone in this particular
imaginary cosmos, although I did not presume that it was the
only such cosmos. I did not think of this.

Looking back on it I can see that the Christian teaching on

God, the angels (and demons), and the individual soul, as interpreted to a child of three years old by his Catholic family, priests and nuns in East Galway towards the end of the First World War, had some part to play in the building of such a *Weltanschauung*. Although the Great Being seemed more impersonal than the Christian God, and his agents more insubstantial than guardian angels or the wicked spirits, who (according to the prayers of Pope Leo XIII recited aloud at the end of Mass) 'wander through the world for the ruin of souls', yet a child might be influenced by one picture in the construction of another. I was on trial. Failure involved punishment. Could God both love and punish what He made? I could not answer.

Ireland was then in a ferment. The sequel to the Easter Rising of 1916 was the gradual withdrawal of much of the population from co-operation with British Rule, the establishment of Self-Rule (*Sinn Féin*) through an independent Assembly (*Dáil*) and courts, and, in reaction, the British use of the notorious Black and Tans and Auxiliaries to intimidate the people into submission. I was certainly frightened by the threatening soldiers. It was not merely that I remember rushing from the narrow dusty roads, and climbing desperately with my mother or my aunt over the low walls or fences to escape the attention of the rampaging Tans in their noisy tenders; but I saw a sturdy blacksmith being pulled by them from a lorry at the end of a rope along the stony village square. This happened after Mass on Sunday, when the operation would be seen by most and have most effect upon the people. He was later dumped in a river two miles away. And I remember a troop of Auxiliaries riding into the town with a ferocious swagger and, although I must have been no more than about six years of age at the time, being among those who carried buckets of water for their horses to drink. The children led a military life too. As our seniors did, so we drilled and practised signalling in the fields, carried rounds of spent ammunition in our bandoleers, and engaged in battles with stones. This psychological environment cannot but have contributed to excitement, at least, and make-believe.

But the pressure at home was, perhaps, greater. My father, Patrick, whose father, also called Patrick, had crossed the Shannon from the island of Ilaunmore on Lough Derg into East Galway, had just started a business in the village of Eyrecourt when, at the age of thirty-three, he died. My mother, Mary Donelan, was about nineteen at the time, bearing her second child, my brother, who was born within seven weeks. Shortly afterwards her younger brother was killed fighting in Dublin on Easter Monday 1916. Her mother died young in the flu of 1918. My mother had to have a serious operation in Dublin which necessitated a stay there for a number of months. Her sister came from London to look after her two infants. Our home was raided by the Tans on a number of occasions, the floor-boards torn up and furniture broken in the vain search for guns. My aunt became the 'mother' of the family, remaining with us all her life, whilst my mother had to look after affairs, which she did with increasing success. But the strain of those harrowing years left her highly nervous. As life went on her nervousness became less.

My mother's condition made it more difficult for her to cope with me for I constantly got into trouble. This greatly excited her so that, certainly as I grew older, she punished me quite severely from time to time. This induced in me some brooding and some solitariness that made me feel miserable and alone. All the same I admired my mother for her looks, her ability, her courage, her devotion to us and her love. She had flattering offers of remarriage, especially from a family friend, who pressed his claim year after year (much to the approval of her children); but she was determined to make a life on her own for herself and her family. She was ambitious; she did not however break free from the tight restraints that frustrated that ambition. In the meantime, although I felt at ease with my aunt who was a placid, affectionate, totally dependent and wholly unambitious person, I could not but continue to think of myself as somewhat isolated, being on trial, and failing to do what I should do. Solipsism endured, even if I was not always conscious of it.

One knows that ideas of another, generally unseen but truly real, world are far from being uncommon. But one wonders if the imaginative propensities of the Celts, a people relegated over the last two thousand years to the fringes of Europe, and long in subjection to other peoples, may not have sought insistently some release in the apprehension of a world other than and a refuge from this. Saga and myth in ancient Ireland implied the existence of a spirit folk that dwelt normally unseen by men in the hills beside them. They are the *áes síde* of Old Irish tradition, known in spoken Irish as the *slua sí* and in English as the fairies. They lived either in certain hills or in far-away islands, or beneath the waters of the sea or of lakes. To the learned they were known as the *Túatha Dé Donann* (later Dannan), the Peoples of the Goddess Donu. Sometimes they were historicized as the former occupiers of Ireland defeated by the invading Goídil or Gaels. Fairies could be active in our lives and could be both good and evil.

Then there are the *Immrama*, a genre of Irish literature describing voyages in the discovery of *Tír na nÓg*, the *Tír Tairngire*, the Promised Land, the land of heart's desire, and (in Christian terms) the Promised Land of the Saints. There were secular and ecclesiastical versions of these journeys with considerable overlapping in contents, even in relation to the kind of heaven to be gained.

The most famous of these *Immrama* is the *Voyage of St Brendan*, my translation of which was beautifully published by the Dolmen Press in 1976. The voyage was conceived by Brendan at Clonfert on the Shannon, his major monastic foundation, part of my native parish. Brendan and his companions are accompanied on the last stage of his journey by a personage (angel?) whom he calls a steward:

The steward went to the front of the boat and showed them the way. When the forty days were up, as the evening drew on, a great fog enveloped them, so that one of them could hardly see another. The steward, however, said to Saint Brendan:

'Do you know what fog this is?'

Saint Brendan replied:

'What?'

Then the other said:

'That fog encircles the island for which you have been searching for seven years.'

After the space of an hour a mighty light shone all around them again and the boat rested on the shore.

On disembarking from the boat they saw a wide land full of trees bearing fruit as in autumn time. When they had gone in a circle around that land, night had still not come on them. One day they came upon a great river flowing through the middle of the island. A youth met them and embraced them with joy and, calling each by his name, said:

'There before you lies the land which you have sought for a long time. You could not find it immediately because God wanted to show you his varied secrets in the great ocean.'

The description of the promised land is something of an anti-climax. Time was suspended there: there was no night, no hunger, no fatigue. But the marvellous incidents of the voyage itself, which take up almost the whole of the narrative, make up the real story: this was a series of trials in which angels and devils guided the action. The concentration was on getting there, on dealing with agents and appearances – with a devil that had possessed a fellow monk, a soporific well, a coagulated sea, a devouring beast, a gryphon, a crystal pillar in the ocean, a fiery mountain, and so much more.

The foregoing reflections may help in understanding why Platonism later became a natural attraction for me: the notion of two worlds, a real world of Intelligence and a shadow world of sense, in which latter we are at present enmeshed. The body is our tomb. Let us assert our *nous*, our intelligence, our true self, and seek union with Intelligence. Neoplatonism – a revival of Platonism (with some accretions) by Plotinus in the third century – was particularly appealing. One may note that a most remarkable translation into English of Plotinus' *Enneads*, six groups each made up of nine essays, was done by the Irishman Stephen MacKenna, and that one of the great exponents of Neoplatonism in modern times, Eric Dodds, formerly Regius Professor of Greek in Oxford, was also Irish – as are a disproportionately high number of more recent academics working in this field.

In the meantime I grew up in a rather dreamy environment. Eyrecourt, as Ida Gantz tells us in *Signpost to Eyrecourt* (1975), to which I am indebted for much of what follows, drew its name from the Eyre family which originated, it was said, at the battle of Hastings. William the Conqueror, having been flung from his horse and suffering suffocation from his displaced helmet, was rescued by a Norman soldier called Truelove. Thereupon, according to the legend, William renamed him 'Eyre, because thou hast given me the "air" I breathe'. Eyre lost his leg and thigh in the battle, whence the thigh and leg appear on the Eyre coat of arms. William gave him lands in Derbyshire. Much later Charlotte Brontë was to find some of her inspiration for *Jane Eyre* in North Lees Hall on the Derbyshire-Yorkshire border, one of the earliest of the Eyre properties.

In due course Eyres appear in Wiltshire and it is from these, from Brickworth, that two sons, John and Edward, came to Ireland in the service of Cromwell around 1650. The efforts of the elder, John, were rewarded with a grant of land which he was allowed to retain at the Restoration. He lived first in the palace of the dispossessed Catholic Bishop of St Brendan's See at Clonfert, a place occupied in the early fifties by Sir Oswald Mosley. Having consolidated an estate of some 30,000 acres, largely in Galway, but also in Offaly and Tipperary, he built his house, known later as Eyrecourt Castle, in the district of *Donanaghta* ('the fort of the breast'), the name now used (*Dún an Ochta*) in Irish for Eyrecourt. This was in the early 1660s. The house survived until after its auction in 1926 when its new owner, being interested only in the land that went with it, allowed it to fall gradually into ruins. I was in it a few times when the Eyres still lived there and later, with grave risk, often ran up one of its crumbling stairs to view the countryside from its unprotected roof.

The demesne and village were the *mise en scène* of my early life. The public had almost full access to the former. This, by now much reduced, lay on the sunny slopes of Redmount Hill (422 feet high) in the direction of the Shannon, which spread out to encompass many islands at Meelick some two miles away. In the distance one could see the Slieve Bloom mountains, often in a blue haze. Before the castle lay a large undulating park with occasional spreading trees. There, within sight of the great house, young men of the village played hurling, hitting the leather ball at what seemed to a small boy, imprudently participating, bewildering speed. To the east of the park, beside the Great Gate that led to Banagher and Birr, was a fox covert, where the followers of the East Galway hounds, now including some Catholic priests and 'strong' farmers, met from time to time. Behind the castle was a wood mainly of beech trees, but with some ash and hazel scrub, springs, a river, an ornamental pond, and a formal garden. I spent many happy hours wandering through the soggy ash scrub and the more open beechwood where the ground was covered in season with snowdrops, daffodils, bluebells and anemones. Near the castle, over the ornamental pond (which thereby suffered badly), there was a very large heronry, swaying recklessly on the top of the beeches in high winds. For a period I counted the herons each year for a society engaged in making a national inventory of these and other less common birds. But my most exciting experience in this wood was coming upon an old postern door beside overgrown yews in a high wall. I pulled myself up to look through the rusty grill at the top. There I gazed upon the formal garden with its heavy-smelling box hedges, herbaceous border and plum trees. They were all rather untidy, it is true, but I thought I had stumbled upon Paradise, a 'walled-in place' of pleasure. On that breath-less occasion I also felt that I was on my own, but that for some reason unknown to me I was being rewarded, or, maybe, tempted.

The castle itself was a minor great house, the main part of which was of two stories with a dormer storey in the sloping roof. There was a pediment over the main, north-facing, entrance which contained a door in a large and quite unusual wooden frame. Over the door was inscribed 'Welcome to the House of Liberty'. The builder of the house, John Eyre I, may have had in mind the liberty from royal oppression maintained by his Wiltshire father (although Charles II is alleged to have danced in Eyrecourt Castle). John Wesley, who visited and preached in Eyrecourt many times, asked uncertainly if it meant liberty from sin? The mullioned windows were later said to have been of Waterford glass.

Internally there were a few fine rooms, including the salon, a ball-room and a dining-room, in the centre of the remarkable ceiling of which was a Tudor rose, to remind guests that conversation here was confidential, *sub rosa*.

But the *pièce de résistance* in Eyrecourt Castle was the truly noteworthy staircase. This approached the first storey from the end of the hall in two flights which came together at a landing and continued as one to the floor above. It was carved of chestnut and oak in Holland, with pedestals carrying vases of fruit and foliage, painted, it is said (but this is not my recollection), in pastel shades. It was the wonder of Connacht.

I well recall that after the auction it was taken to pieces over a period of several months by a bowler-hatted Cockney, put in packing-cases, and then shipped to America, ultimately to the Detroit Institute of Arts. There it remained, unpacked, at least fifty years later.

John Wesley, having admitted that the staircase was grand, as were two or three of the rooms, remarked on the ruinous outhouses and other appointments as seeming to indicate the owner's apathy. The owner then, in 1775, was John Eyre, Baron Eyre of Eyrecourt since 1768, and a member of the Privy Council which effectively ruled Ireland. The family had reached its greatest glory. But Baron Eyre had no issue and his life ended sadly in 1781. Richard Cumberland in his *Memoirs*, published in 1807, describes his declining years:

His Lordship's day was so apportioned as to give the afternoon by much the largest share of it, during which, from an early dinner to the hour of rest, he never left his chair, nor did the claret ever quit the table. This did not produce inebriety, for it was sipping rather than drinking that filled up the time, and this mechanical process of gradually moistening the human clay was carried on with very little aid from conversation, for his lordship's companions were not very communicative, and fortunately he was not very curious. He lived in an enviable independence as to reading, and, of course, he had no books. Not one of the windows of his castle was made to open, but luckily he had no liking for fresh air, and the consequence may be better conceived than described.

One window on the ground floor, at least, opened by 1926, for I went in and out through it from an overfull auction room. I do not recollect a library or the presence of many books.

Some of the Eyres over the centuries had a little education; some of them had great fortunes; and clearly some of them had taste. But generally they concentrated rather on sport, hunting, dancing and social entertainment, and so sometimes found themselves short of funds. The most notorious of them was Giles Eyre, who had £20,000 a year, wasted £80,000 on an election (which he lost) in Galway and spent years in a debtors' prison. He is the original of Charles Lever's *Charles O'Malley*:

> *To drink a toast*
> *A proctor roast,*
> *Or bailiff as the case is,*
> *To kiss your wife*
> *Or take a life*
> *At ten or fifteen paces,*
> *To keep game-cocks, to hunt the fox*
> *To drink in punch the Solway,*
> *With debts galore, but fun far more —*
> *Oh! that's 'The Man for Galway'.*

Giles Eyre was illiterate. The estate, which grew to 85,000 acres at one period, was leased and sold in various portions at one time or another, until in the end no more than a few hundred acres went with the castle. Fecklessness had left a romantic fantasy of neglect and ruins. This was the sensuous background to my dawning years. When last I saw the castle, fat bullocks were congregating before the House of Liberty defiling its granite steps.

To the west of the demesne developed the village which came to be known as Eyres' Court. An avenue lined with elms beside a ruined church, built by the first John Eyre and where Giles Eyre is buried, leads through an unpretentious gate out into the Mall and thence to the gently curved Main Street, which is distinguished in having a large number of three-storey Georgian houses, of which ours was one. They must originally have been built for various Agents of the Estate. Some six of these in the village were in my young days in total ruins, exciting and dangerous areas as playgrounds for hide-and-seek and other vigorous games. Two buildings stood out among all others, the house used by the parish priest and the theatre, known locally as the Synagogue. The former was distinguished not only by elaborate entrance steps and pillars crowned by eagles: it also had a 'hanging' garden, suspended on high arches, at the back. There the Big Man, as the parish priest was known both familiarly and in fear, regaled me once in a hammock with oranges and a honeycomb. The house also had a painted ceiling (which, naturally, was alleged to have been done by Angelica Kaufmann) and a curved corridor leading into the organ loft of the nearby chapel, a corridor sometimes used for storing wool. This house once belonged to the Martyn family, of whom Edward was a friend of W. B. Yeats and a collaborator in the Irish Literary Renaissance at the beginning of the century. The house faced the broad Market Square which had two plots of grass and two large trees with high circular stone surrounds. A theatre was built here, a miniature in cut limestone of what a theatre should be: a Parterre with benches upholstered in red cloth; behind it a Pit for those who stood only; and above this a Gallery for the 'Gods' with plain wooden benches. The stage with its flies and curtain, painted with a scene from the *Colleen Bawn*, were of proportionate size, and there was a decent dressing-room. Here were held plays and films (I remember only Charlie Chaplin) and concerts, in one of which I played on the piano a piece called 'Corps de Ballet', the pronounced rhythm of which provoked such time-beating in the feet of the audience that the piece could hardly be heard even by me. Later the slate roof of the Synagogue fell in and the building became a zinc-roofed dance-hall. The Big Man, disapproving of its clients who came there from outside the parish, put a short end to the dancing by parading up and down outside the door with his blackthorn stick. That was the way it was!

As for the rest of the village: it was a jumble of houses with an interesting roofscape as one entered it from the east by the low, broad-and-grassy-margined road that hugged the crumbling demesne wall (a place well suited for courting couples, and equally well patrolled by the parish priest). The Protestant graveyard was beside its church, neatly kept: even the graves when open were lined with moss and violets. The Catholic graveyard lay beside the old church of Donanaghta, several fields in from the road over a bumpy frequently sodden track, and filled with soaring nettles. It was called Doon (I thought the name was 'Doom'), an eerie place.

The countryside around had its share of bogs, stone walls, fields little and great of mixed quality land, but the chief attraction in the area was the Shannon, two or three miles distant. Here the greatest river of the British Isles split up among many islands. There were gentle falls obviated for navigation purposes by a large weir, a canal and lock-gates. Over this pleasant scene presided a Martello tower erected against a Napoleonic attack, occupied by the Free State soldiers during the Civil War of 1922-3, and a ruined Franciscan convent going back to 1414, of which the rambling and austere church was still in use. George Petrie in the last century remarked upon the 'romantic situation' of the Abbey. Here, at Meelick, from my earliest days I engaged in every kind of fishing: for perch and roach from the banks and weir with a worm; trolling from boats with a sprat or spinner for pike or with fly for trout or salmon. How I remember the excitement of a cork dipping firmly to a bite; or hauling in one young pike after another when a run was on; but especially trout rising all around one at the weir at midnight and the moon lighting up the poop of the boat as one rowed drowsily homewards. This was O'Madden country. Eyrecourt Castle was built beside an O'Madden tower; Meelick Abbey had been refounded by the O'Madden chief in 1479 and nearby was Lismore, one of the fortresses of the O'Maddens. It was appropriately a Father Madden, a nearby parish priest, who brought me fly-fishing in company with another cleric, who spoke constantly of books and in particular of Horace (whose *Odes* he had translated), an author whom I was to get to know somewhat better quite soon.

Meelick seemed to be another country. On warm sunny days one saw the fat bream approach, but rarely bite, in the shallow water. One smelt the sedge and mint and meadowsweet as one brushed through the long grass. Yellow irises were everywhere and, occasionally, white lilies in the pools. And over the flat sweet-smelling, purple-heathered bogland lay the pale blue range of Slieve Bloom. Here I sometimes stopped still, overcome by the sudden feeling that I was part of nature, happy to be one with it, at ease in having lost a human, personal identity, free from relations save submission to the experience of the earth. Later I was to read so much more of this in Forrest Reid and Richard Jefferies. Then I was only half-conscious of such fleeting thoughts. But I have other, more troubling recollections of that place: of a young Free State soldier being shot in an ambush there, and his body lying in a tender outside our house, to be viewed by his girl-friend, our maid. Indeed Free State officers were often in our house, their Mauser rifles stacked in a corner in the kitchen.

The physical furnishing of our lives then belonged, understandably, largely to the nineteenth century. The footpaths were cobbled, the roads unmetalled, the streets unlit except where a shop window shed a fitful brightness from the paraffin lamp inside. The post came to the village and went by gig, which took passengers to the train at Ballinasloe. There were few motor-cars and they constantly broke down or suffered punctures from the sharp stones that filled the innumerable pot-holes. These were broken by men with hammers and goggles sitting on the heaps of stone beside the road. Cyclists, if ever they lit their way, used sizzling carbide lamps. Poor people, the majority, bought almost totally fat American bacon and Indian meal ('Injun male'): how close the Great Famine lingered. The children were often barefoot, but often by choice in summer. It was wonderful to leave off one's canvas sandals to experience the soft warm feeling of the sandy road.

The tragedies and eccentricities of life were less contained than now. I've heard the terrible wails of a woman being brought forcibly from her home, doubtless forever, to the madhouse. I've seen a man die in the heaving fever of tuberculosis, while his wife ironed the sheets for his laying-out in the kitchen next door. I attended very many wakes, where I said how sorry I was for 'their trouble' and at least once was offered a white clay pipe and twist tobacco. I attended even more funerals, which frequently started with the placing of the coffin on chairs outside the house in the street, where a decade of the Rosary was said. Sometimes with other small boys I made my way sociably from one trap to another throughout the length of a long funeral procession. Fun tended to break in on sorrow. There were all kinds of curious people about, local and visiting: a butcher in the D.T.s, a pale-faced poet, an old man who moaned out loud in sympathy with Christ's Passion in the darkened chapel (but who for all that eventually got married in a nearly ribald ceremony at the altar). There's nothing like a village for seeing life. Then one saw even more of it.

Widowhood and spinsterhood hung oppressively over the Main Street. On our side of it, over a stretch of six consecutive houses, there were four widows and two sets of three bachelors or spinsters. The Vanishing Irish. Pleasure, glorified, was for the next life. Still, the local church did not force-feed with piety. The parish priest was a big rough man, who always kept to the middle of the street, always had a Kerry Blue terrier about, even during Mass, always dribbled and spat copiously from snuff-taking, preached dramatically in alternative *pianissimo* and *fortissimo* and then *da capo*, read out the list of seasonal collections for his upkeep from £5 down to sixpence, with threats to publicize the names of those who did not contribute at all. He had the doors of the chapel closed half-way through Mass, and then at the end of the ceremony marched boldly down the aisle to open half of the main door, hold the collection plate over his portly belly, and make mock-threatening remarks or gestures to the faithful as they made their way singly out, dropping their intermittent pennies. He had the local reputation of being the richest man in Connacht though it can hardly have been so. He did nothing to make himself loved. His piety was straightforward and simple. He depended upon visiting 'missioners' to whip up the annual ecstasies of devotion.

A few other clerics conduced even less to piety. One curate was an alcoholic who frequently made the rounds of the Stations of the Cross in Lent in a half-drunken stupor and had to be helped to his feet from time to time by the altar-boys, who did not discourage him from saying more than the ten Hail Marys to the decade when he came to recite the Rosary. Being so unfortunate, it was thought appropriate that he should be compensated by being able to work cures. Certainly some sufferers were brought from long distances to have him read an Office over them. Eventually he was silenced by the Bishop for some time, and died suddenly after he had been reinstated. A priest from one local parish was thought to be interested only in his big horse, Black Jack. Another had a kennel of greyhounds, kept by a man and woman who were notorious for their bad language. There were other clergy in the area who were conspicuously good pastors. But when one contemplated a collection of priests murdering the Office at a Requiem Mass, with their yellowing creased surplices, one felt that religion was indifferently represented.

Religion was more effectively communicated in the schools. My recollection of the nuns' Convent School (where I suffered the comparative isolation of being advanced, with one other boy, into the girls' section because I was still too young to go to the all boys' school) is of hymn-singing, *Agnus Deis* (little religious objects), and selling Black Babies in Africa to those who paid pennies to stick pins in little squares: these were arranged in the form of a cross on a paper card. From there also

I made my First Communion in a white woollen suit. When I got to the Boys' or Master's School, religion, curiously, became more serious. There, although religious instruction was supposed to be given only when a notice, 'Religious Instruction', was turned face upwards from noon to 12.30 p.m., I became conscious of more indoctrination. There was more hymn-singing, in which I took immense pleasure, both in the music and the words. I was taught how to serve Mass and lisp the difficult responses in Latin, a language of which I was destined to know more: *Quia tu es, Deus, fortitudo mea: quare me repulisti, et quare tristis incedo, dum affligit me inimicus?* Not only did we have to know the 'large' Maynooth Catechism, which formulated so many inscrutable mysteries, by heart, but we had to know and be able to 'explain' everything from a thick, small, closely printed Explanatory Catechism as well. I got great satisfaction in 'mastering' this: that is, in effect, with my mother's instant help having it off by heart. This intense instruction was aimed at satisfying each year a Diocesan Examiner, who relieved us always by asking us only to sing the hymns, and the Bishop when we came before him for Confirmation. The latter contented himself with giving us a pat on the cheek. The Master's anxiety, however, was so great to prepare for these examinations (he was employed by the parish priest) that he fell into some sadism from time to time. A number of the 'scholars' as they were called (a survival of the time when few had formal education) were not particularly bright and, perhaps, not overly industrious. When they missed questions, the Master directed that they be slapped with a switch, cut from a hedge outside the school, by the boy that answered best. It was a brutalizing experience for all, and in the name of religion. When Confirmation came and these backward boys were not presented by the Master to the Bishop, the Big Man slipped them in at the rails, and all was well. Such is the difficulty that a clergy, which on occasion indeed drives too hard, has in keeping in touch with a simple-minded and enthusiastic laity.

The Master, in fact, was a very pleasant man in the normal way. He worked under almost impossible conditions. His modest apprentice-training had not prepared him to teach the Irish language. Yet certain educational pundits had assured the new Irish Government after 1922 that the desired revival of Irish could be achieved in some five years or so. Crash courses in the language were held for primary school teachers during the summer months. Our Master, being no longer young, made slow progress with these; he evidently did not have his heart in the venture. His attempts, therefore, to teach what became a central subject were pathetic, which much reduced his self-esteem before the knowing 'scholars'. In any case he was the sole teacher in a school in which there normally averaged (he took the roll and chalked up the number present each day) twenty-two boys, divided into six classes, these being taken two by two. He could do no more than give instructions to each group what to learn, or appoint a boy from an upper group to teach a lower. He was content to keep a general and amused eye on one or two retarded youths who stayed in school well into their late teens. This gave him plenty of time to talk with the woman whose family shared the building with the school. Indeed the school used only one room and the hall on the ground floor of a large house. It was squalid beyond belief. The Master constantly got cups of tea from the woman through an unintended but convenient hole in a latticed partition wall. There were not enough desks even for the small attendance, and these were infested with lice and vermin whose antics afforded us distraction. The 'library' was a row of some twenty unpretentious and dust-laden volumes on the mantelpiece over a frequently smoking open turf fire. The scholars contributed the turf and were allowed to warm themselves, singly, standing at the fire when they got too cold. There was no covering on the floor which was splashed with water (to keep down the dust) and swept by a boy every day. The dado of the walls was painted in the darkest green imaginable, and for a foot or so under the ceiling there was a 'cacophony' of small pieces of wallpaper taken from a book of samples.

Here the Master did his best for us. It is amazing what children can learn on their own, especially if somebody sympathetic 'hears' them. We, or at least some of us, were constantly doing examinations, especially in arithmetic, algebra and Euclid. I can testify that I learned enough mathematics in that school to bring me easily through the general paper in that subject in the first year in university. I still recollect long sessions with my companions matching the details of a geography textbook against maps of Great Britain and pre-1914 Europe. English literature and poetry inculcated a love of country and the countryside:

> Go ye round Erin, gaze upon her loveliness;
> Lake lands and gorse lands, they all may claim a share.
> Heather lands and meadow-lands, mountain heights and lowlands –
> Ah, God was good to Ireland when He moulded her so fair.

After appropriate verses on Kerry, we came happily to Galway:

> Turn ye to Westward, behold the cliffs of Galway;
> Grey, stern and glorious, those bulwarks of the West.

I do not know who composed these modest, but to us moving, verses, nor have I seen them printed anywhere since. But they and ballad songs and books about the history of Ireland filled us with an abiding love of the land in which we were born.

There was no visiting library or bookshop in Eyrecourt. American comic-cuts, 'Mutt and Jeff', 'Tillie the Toiler', 'The Katzenjammer Kids' and so on came weekly from emigrants in Boston and were avidly devoured and passed on. A visit to

Dublin meant a stocking up with cheap reprints of popular novels then available in Woolworths. I had an additional source in a Miss Alice Butson, a middle-aged invalid, who visited the village from her house near Clonfert weekly in a donkey and trap and, while her driver did messages, passed on to me such books as she thought would interest me. It was a vein of gold.

As I approached my teens it was felt that I had got as much as I could from the local school. My maternal grandmother had been a boarder at a convent of *La Sainte Union*, and a former neighbour and, it was alleged, 'admirer' of my father was also a member of that congregation: hence plans were afoot to send me to Kilashee, a preparatory school in Co. Kildare. In the event my widowed mother found it difficult to let me go away from her. I continued, then, with the Master until I was thirteen.

One other element in my schooling comes to be mentioned, music. My earliest remembrance of singing goes back to the preparation of a song, 'Cill Mhuire', for a Feis, when I was almost six. I was summoned back in the final of the contest to be dazzled by the footlights and bewildered by the darkness beyond. I was frightened and felt lost as to what I was doing. Still, I got a prize, as my brother and myself did for step-dancing on that occasion too. The prizes were books of Irish song and grammar from which youths of sixteen and over, if they were determined, might with difficulty have drawn some profit. There was much singing of hymns and patriotic ballads in my school, and from our gramophone records I built up a strong collection of post-Great War and twenties songs and ditties. Among the patriotic ballads I knew was:

Up with de Valera, he's the champion of the right –
We'll follow him to battle, 'neath the orange, green, and white,
Next we'll tackle England and we'll beat her in the fight,
And we'll crown de Valera King of Ireland.

This we schoolboys sang rather uncertainly. To some of my cousins de Valera was a hero; to my own family, anathema, because of whatever responsibility he had for the Civil War. My brother and myself treated whoever of the village was within earshot to a frequent rendering of our repertoire of songs (reflecting many and not infrequently competing interests) when we were put to bed, while it was yet light, in the summertime.

One's imagination was stimulated in so many ways. The countryside was full of raths where, we half believed, the fairies lived. The empyrean was lit up on winter nights by the moon sailing through scuddying white clouds: it was a witching time when forms – a man on a bicycle, a wandering goat – revealed themselves suddenly against a dark background of trees. Even during daytime a tiny aeroplane very high up in the sky seemed like a cross appearing noisily in the heavens. Of course when one believed that God, in the visible form of the Eucharistic wafer reserved in the tabernacle on the altar in the chapel, was really present, one was sensitized powerfully towards the perception of a world other than this one pervading every moment of one's existence. There was the minor but equally constant presence of one's guardian angel, just over one's shoulder. The true enduring reality was the unseen. What we saw and did was changeable. And so fantasy was born. Night after night, instead of composing ourselves for sleep, my brother and myself created plays or 'stories' (as we called them) in which we spoke the dialogue of many parts. Our enthusiasm for invention was restrained, and a happy conclusion to the story suddenly imposed, by my mother's banging with clear intent upon the separating wall. That put an end to our histrionics.

TWO

Shades of the prison-house begin to close
Upon the growing Boy

EVENTUALLY I had to leave my sleepy village and go to boarding-school. Rockwell College in County Tipperary was chosen, partly because it had at the time an outstanding record of success in public examinations, but mostly, I feel, because a friend of my mother had been a pupil there at the turn of the century. It was a school run by the Holy Ghost Fathers who had come from France to Tipperary via Blackrock College in Dublin. The estate which they occupied had seen two members of its recent owners done to death in retribution for evictions they had made. The property came to the Holy Ghost Fathers from Monsieur Charles Thiebault, a resident of Dundee, who wished them to found a seminary for the education of priests for Scotland and do whatever other things the Congregation, which later at any rate had strong missionary commitments, might wish. Hence Rockwell, founded in 1864, was initially known as the 'Scotch' College, sister to the 'French' College, Blackrock, in Dublin.

The French priests were enchanted with their new home: they found it 'too splendid' with its space, its lake, its woods and its fields all set in the Golden Vale against the dramatic background of the Galtee Mountains.

By the 5th of September 1928, when I got there, Rockwell had greatly developed, but had still, as many other schools had then, a strong imprint, physical and moral, of the comparative hardships of the nineteenth century. Plumbing was neither efficient nor extensive. On getting up in the morning a dormitory of perhaps thirty boys washed in chipped enamel basins, filled from a central cold tap and in due course emptied into a wooden trough. As the trough filled with the soapy water the basins bobbed to and fro as one washed, until at last the scholastic in charge (a young man training for the priesthood in the Congregation) removed a bung from the trough to fill a large bucket. This was then emptied into the single, already overworked, toilet. The tables in the refectory were covered with white oilcloth, worn to its brown base in places. Tea was served to a table of some dozen boys from a central metal urn in which saccharine had already been put and, for some meals, milk. Bread came in four-pound gooey loaves. The meat was nearly always unbled mutton with blue veins; the vegetables were turnips and parsnips that gave one heartburn. We need not pursue these matters further. We took them fatalistically for granted. Improvements were to come.

The moral discipline was severe too. We had study before breakfast to which we proceeded in single file, supposedly in silence, along the side of a near-quadrangle, while scholastics stationed along the way urged us on with the half-sporting threat of blows from the hard wooden knob at the end of their long swinging cinctures. After breakfast we were herded in a walk of a mile or so around the lake without coats or caps no matter how cold it was, an exhilarating experience with lovely vistas of the mountains. If the day were wet most of the boys circled a corridor, necessarily in one direction. Likewise when we walked on the 'track' in the playing-fields outside, we had to do the same. The scholastics could not be friendlier, but it was a 'warder' system. Again, it was taken for granted.

The teaching, for bright boys, was pretty intense. They were put in relatively small classes, given the best teachers, and kept in doing Greek and Latin Verse for part of the time assigned to recreation for the school as a whole. On the other hand boys who were not bright at all were treated very humanely indeed. The bulk of the boys were encouraged by some caning, ordered by the master in class and administered by a Dean who was as aware of the propensities of the master as of the boys. There was also a system of weekly assessments or Notes, read out before the whole school assembled before the President. If one fared more than usually badly, the President, known as 'Busty', was apt to call out with thunderous rumblings, 'Stand up, you abominable boy.' It was a severe ordeal for some. The hardened boys, however, basked rather in such 'glory'. There was an Honours List too which, additionally, was posted up for all to see.

Religion in the school was taken for granted, an active but discreet background to our lives. This was natural, since almost without exception the boys came from families of more or less ardent Catholics. We sang some nice hymns in chapel, one of which spoke to our amusement of the beautiful feet of the missionaries which our teachers hoped to be. More moving was the 'Veni Sancte Spiritus' (the Fathers were of the Congregation of the Holy Ghost) which in Latin and in Gregorian chant is to me a most moving hymn, touching at once our highest hopes and greatest needs.

It was in Rockwell that, as I remember, I first made up my mind to aspire to the priesthood. The contrast between these Holy Ghost priests and scholastics on the one hand and the clergy at the time in the diocese of Clonfert greatly impressed me, not that some of the former did not show disappointing weaknesses too. The ranks of young men in their surplices and birettas in the chancel stalls invited one to join them in the most noble of all vocations. To what more worthy object could one devote one's life than the service of man in the following of Christ, *of God*? The answer left no room whatever for doubt. None. How could one *possibly* resist such a call? Unless one felt

oneself a blackguard and resigned to doing evil, one had no
choice but to follow *God*. Only the Devil said no to God. But
it seemed to me that if I were to become a *good* priest, I should
do so in my own native diocese, where, I thought, I might be
useful. It was not the piety of the college priests that affected
me, for they were not notably pious. It was the simple
acceptance that there was a God, invisible, Whom one should
serve as best one could. A priest did so in a professional way.
What little sense of what is normally considered to be reality!
The material world still was secondary to me.

In my first term I was with one older boy cast in a farce
called *The Courting of Mary Doyle* which was hawked around the
neighbouring towns to make money for the African Mission of
the Holy Ghost Fathers. I played the part of a twenties flapper
with cloche hat and short tight silky black dress: this I found
inconvenient when I yielded to the urge to jump over the backs
of chairs. I do not remember feeling confident in the role, but
it didn't matter, since I was but accessory to the farce which
went beyond all bounds in response to avid audiences. There
was much rehearsal for this play which took place in the private
room of one of the teaching staff. He, unfortunately, was more
interested in this flapper than was comfortable for her, and
made advances that were turned ingenuously aside. But my
friends and I shamelessly devoured the toffees he left frequently
in my desk. Later this man got into more serious difficulties and
left the college. He was not the only embarrassing pursuer.
These torrid 'friendships' were then obtrusive in the place but
I do not believe that there were any homosexual practices
involved. All during study, notes passed through a succession
of hands to and fro from senior boys to junior, being read (and
often glossed) by the boys between. I reported my own
experience to my mother during the first vacation. I observed
that she felt powerless to deal with the situation beyond telling
me to speak to the Prefect of Studies. I cannot remember if I

did this, but, if I did, I noted no change.

I was not greatly shocked by all this. Growing up in a country village I saw little sophistication, but I did see the manifestations of nature, particularly animal nature. *Nil admirari*, paradoxically, was easy to practise. There was something else too. A weak sense of the reality of things exempted one from being too much engaged in them. Things happened to you anyway: there was no need to react too much. Later a saying of Emerson was to mean much to me: justify yourself to yourself, and do not concern yourself with the opinion of others. There is something solipsistic here too.

I have many happy memories of Rockwell: of practising Beethoven with Father Nepomecene Müller, who was reported to have only half a lung; of joining in chorus with his compatriot Father Schmidt (a little *exalté*) in singing rousing victory songs in the quadrangle when the College won a rugby match; of singing at soirées; of racing in a skiff on the lake; of the luxury of 'library' time in the last three-quarters of an hour before going to bed. I fell under the spell of Robert Hugh Benson and his stories of heroic Jesuits during religious persecution in England.

The time came, however, when, if I were to aim at the priesthood in my native diocese, I should transfer to its seminary. Moreover, as my younger brother had at this time to embark on secondary education also, it was convenient for my widowed mother to have us near home. To Garbally then I came in September 1930.

* * *

The diocesan seminary, which was in practice a rather normal secondary boarding-school, occupied the former residence and estate of the Earls of Clancarty, owners of the town of Ballinasloe, famous for its October Horse Fairs, on the river Suck. Apart from class and study, which were conducted in the refurbished buildings of a classic stone-cut stable-yard, the boys slept and ate and went to chapel in the great house itself some short distance away. This too was in the shape of a quadrangle, with a grand portico and pleasant terraces. Although there was the pervading gloom of limestone in a misty climate, the house and extensive ornamental grounds had elegance and grace that elevated the soul.

The school had a reverend President who was distinguished-looking and handsome at any time but especially when, as happened regularly, he rode to hounds on a fine horse in tall hat and with the other conventional hunting accoutrements. He pursued the *comme il faut* in simplicity and seriousness, and although we smiled at his simplicity and disliked his serious-ness, we were ungratefully conscious that he was doing his best for us and that we should benefit from his endeavours. Occasionally on Sunday evenings he assembled us (to the number of 120 or so) in the old Clancarty library, where a brightly burning wood fire animated the ample fireplace. There he stood before us with one slippered foot resting on the tall leather-topped brass fender, and lectured us on etiquette, or gave us middle-brow musical recitals on a gramophone, or got us to sing improving songs such as 'Keep Right On to the End of the Road'. He had a number of influential friends in Dublin whom he got to help his college in various ways. Through them he arranged to have a (weakened) Irish rugby international side play our senior team, or have a Cambridge athletic coach visit us from time to time, or have the Rathmines and Rathgar Opera producer help us with our Gilbert and Sullivan. The altar in the chapel and its furniture was designed by Arthur Power. The Victorian furnishings of the salons were carefully maintained and given limited use. It was hard not to respond a little to such comprehensive efforts to improve us. But they were so persistent as to annoy us. You couldn't pass the President on a path without his telling you, for the hundredth time, in measured rather melancholy tones, to hold yourself straight. Rarely did a furtive smile eventually dawn over his puckered face. Intelligence was said not to be his strong suit. His tendency to righteousness very occasionally led him to take his duty of punishing to what then seemed harsh and would now seem brutal lengths. I have seen him break half a dozen canes before the whole school on the hands of boys whom he judged guilty of some 'serious' transgression. Still I remember him with gratitude for his dedication to our formation.

The other presiding genius of the school was the Matron, Miss Delaney, a smiling rubicund middle-aged woman of generous proportions. She made sure that we got plenty of good appetizing and varied food, served to us by neat maids dressed in black with white apron and cap. There were special treats, as when the Michaelmas goose was carved by the head boy at each table. The Matron was a cheerful motherly woman and not intrusive.

The intellectual diet was of the Classics. There was then little, if indeed any, science taught and no foreign languages. On the other hand the Irish language received considerable, but not altogether unrestrained, emphasis. These features reflected the poor funding of Irish education, which depended very largely on Church bodies to provide and maintain buildings, and to some extent on the surrendered State salaries of the religious teachers to provide subsidized teaching. They also reflected the simplistic drive of the Irish Government to revive Irish, our native language, which had for the most part disappeared. In those days the courses for the public examinations in Irish were rather open and indeed challenging. The language was unfamiliar and complicated and the themes in the literature were, not surprisingly, suppression and unavailing patriotism. Although I was never comfortable in the language, at that time through force of work and inspired teaching I came temporarily within distance of being fluent. I also sported the gold Fáinne (a ring of gold worn on the lapel) which indicated that I was able and willing to speak Irish to all comers. I wore the emblem rightfully for a year or two at university.

I have pleasant recollections of reading Horace's *Odes* with a companion, sitting outside on a first-floor window-sill in the sunshine. The edition (by T. E. Page) I used then lies before me now, and I regret to observe that the 'Ode to Pyrrha' (I.5) was marked as unrequired, that is, not worthy of or, more likely, not suitable for our attention. I read all the *Odes* some four times in my last two years at school. I note from the dates inscribed underneath each ode that I read books one to three during the second half of July 1932, when the competing distraction during this holiday period was to ride a bicycle unendingly in circles on the untarmacadamed village street. The *Odes* did not have in my adolescence the troubling effect I now think they might have had. Lines such as 'while burning love and passion [*libido*], such as goad mares, shall rage around your wounded liver [*jecur*]', apart from some heightened curiosity as to what such phrases as 'my liver swells' really meant, were strengthless against the defences of indoctrination. The world intangible anaesthetized my heart. Even Latin which speaks for ordinary human emotions powerfully, in contrast to the intellectualism and sometimes mysticism of Greek, was diverted for the moment before the conditioning to asceticism. The diversion was to the Roman Missal, to the Liturgy and to Latin hymns. Every morning we followed Mass in Latin relishing the lovely cadences: *Lavabo inter innocentes manus meas . . . ego autem in innocentia mea ingressus sum . . . pes meus stetit in directo; in ecclesiis benedicam te, Domine.* The Gregorian chant was so ethereal and dignified that one was transported as it were into an angelic or at least monastic atmosphere. *Salve Regina . . . vita, dulcedo et spes nostra, salve.* The sublimation was subtle and potent. The senses too were overcome.

The ordinary religious propaganda of the school was raised

while I was there to far greater intensity by a rather unusual Jesuit whose retreats to schools produced a flood of vocations to the priesthood and convents about this time. He had a somewhat strange appearance, combining piercing eyes and a resonant, singsong voice of much emotional range, with an enormously high linen dog-collar, a long black gown with long wings and black slippers with red piping. His favourite quotation from Scripture was: 'The Kingdom of Heaven suffereth violence and the violent bear it away.' The full rigour of asceticism was, as far as he could contrive it, imposed. You took the strongest measures not only against 'temptations' of any kind but positively in pursuit of the following of Christ. Decision was easy. Action had to follow. Becoming a religious of some kind was practically inevitable. Few of my class-mates failed to take his advice. He observed to me on one occasion with satisfaction that a whole class of eighteen girls in one of the convents he visited became nuns. 'Narrow is the gate and strait is the way that leadeth to life; and few there are that find it,' he bellowed constantly. He seemed determined to increase the few.

This priest's particular formula for success in violence was to kneel before the Real Presence, reserved in the tabernacle on the altar in the appearance of a wafer, for a quarter of an hour every day. To some this soon seemed not to be enough. Having rushed down to the chapel to pray before Mass began, assisted at Mass, taken the Eucharist, made a due Thanksgiving, rushed back to the chapel after breakfast to do the quarter of an hour's visit to the Blessed Sacrament before class began, these enthusiasts occupied periods of recreation in saying the Little Office of the Blessed Virgin (once suppressed, with the Jesuits, by the Holy See) which took about ten minutes to get through. They did also the fourteen Stations of the Cross, which took anything up to twenty minutes. In addition there was the public recital of the Rosary followed frequently by Benediction. The day closed with formal night prayers and one's own prayers at one's bedside. Before examinations some recited for thirty days a prayer of inordinate length and less than inevit-able effect with a view to improving results. On Sundays there were, I think, two Masses to attend and from time to time an hour's visit to the Blessed Sacrament. I need hardly say that I now regard such religious endeavour by so many in a school of adolescents as well over the limit of what might be considered desirable. I wonder how the President tolerated such excess: perhaps his own simplicity and serious pursuit of perfection betrayed him. I cannot but believe that others of the priests, who indulged in no such excess of piety, must have had many doubts.

On the other hand our formal classes and examinations in Christian Doctrine were taken with something less than seriousness. During the half-hour devoted to the subject, when we were tired before lunch, the teacher planned strategy for our games of rugby or hurling, drawing diagrams on the blackboard and joking merrily about school news of one kind or another. Only the most perfunctory reference was made to the pre-scribed Scripture and textbooks. There was no discussion of points arising from them. It was assumed that we were untroubled by problems. And indeed there was a blanket, almost unthinking, acceptance of all the formulae. This in itself did reduce the perception of problems. Likewise when the written examination of Christian Doctrine took place, there was a lack of supervision and recourse to copying and cheating that would be unthinkable for secular subjects. There were surprising winners of the prize in Christian Doctrine. This side of religion was taken for granted and as needing little attention.

There was a physical counterpart to this Christian idealism. What time was left over from study and prayer (most of it *not* of obligation) was largely occupied with games. There was little hanging about and no provision for any general reading. We togged out for rugby or, in summer, hurling or tennis, almost every day. We trained hard for athletics and dieted accordingly. We were keen, eager and spare.

But the serpent penetrated even here. Some younger boys smoked; arrangements were provided for the older boys, and those who earned privileges, to smoke, if they wished to, in a special area of the grounds called the Tunnel. There were some innocent crushes between the boys. The Gilbert and Sullivan operettas, for which I played the piano in a small orchestra made up of musicians from the area, stimulated some of this. The sopranos sometimes made rather convincing girls (and sometimes not), decked out in the glory of plumes hired from Dublin.

It is well to bear in mind that the peculiar level of piety practised then by more than a few of the boys in this college is to be placed against the background of the mental aggrandizement of the Church that followed on the independence of the twenty-six counties of the Irish Free State in 1922. With the disappearance of government of the country by Protestant Britain, and the hangers-on of that administration, and the British army, and the Royal Irish Constabulary, the way was open for the Catholic Church to use its influence unfettered. The Church had made possible at great sacrifice the secondary education which a growing section of the population, gradually recovering from the discriminatory laws of earlier centuries, was beginning to need in the nineteenth century. By 1922 the Church dominated the minds of the politicians, civil servants, the professional people and the business community. Whereas before the period 1916-22 a Catholic might ignore or defy his Church and yet get preferment by the British Protestant administration, after 1922 he had to keep his eye on the Church or, even worse, the righteous, sometimes hypocritical, lay-people who were more Catholic than the Bishops.

The Church's influence was quickly felt. Divorce was withdrawn. Fatuous censorship was introduced. A Vocational Education Bill was passed which made it virtually impossible for anyone to enter the professions (and so have influence within the community) without having passed through a Church school. De Valera, having joined in a ruinous civil war in refusal to swear an oath of allegiance to the British monarch, and then, losing that war and the way to power, having pronounced that the oath was an insignificant formality, introduced a new constitution for the State, the undue influence of the Church on which was later recognized. De Valera not only worked hard for the revival of the Irish language (which, if successful, could only have an isolating effect on the people) but also declared economic war on England. There followed the Second World War, in which Ireland cultivated a proclaimed and careful neutrality.

The ideal put before young people during that period was given innocent expression by the Christian Brothers, who educated more students than any other group of religious, in a famous pamphlet called *Éire, Sean is Nua* (Ireland, Old and New). The cover draws inspiration from the rebellion of 1916 and its leader Pádraig Pearse (of English extraction), a mystic who believed that such a blood-sacrifice was needed. Ireland of the future, according to this crude and simple document, was to have all its problems solved: full employment on land and sea, and in factories; the best food products in the world; self-sufficiency; love of Jesus and Mary; no emigration except of missionary priests, nuns and brothers; the Irish language heard everywhere; admiring tourists; and the reunion of the country. Things looked simple to de Valera and the Brothers; but resumed colossal emigration to England in the fifties began the rude awakening from an understandable but dangerous dream.

It is against such an ideological background and under the almost feverish impulse of the ascetic regime, in which I had so easily involved myself, that I agreed with the Jesuit, who had conducted such uncompromising retreats for us, that I should aspire to become a member not of the diocesan clergy but of the

Jesuits, the Society or very Company of Jesus. Another strong influence in that direction was the reading of the life of a Jesuit chaplain, Willie Doyle, in the First World War, written by a self-proclaimed polymath, Alfred O'Rahilly, once a Jesuit scholastic and afterwards President of University College, Cork, a person for whom I had later qualified admiration. Willie Doyle's life was heroic and inspiring.

In the meantime school life absorbed the rest of my attention. My teacher of English recommended me to read Macaulay to develop style. I read him religiously (the correct word) with intense boredom for one hour every evening in the finely bound volumes of the Clancarty library. Daily I fell asleep over his banal lucidity. And yet such prolonged exposure to a particular, and admittedly successful, style, must have had some effect. Similarly my equally relentless repetition of Horace's *Odes* could not have been without result. At any rate I had a satisfactory result in English in my final examination and fared equally well in the subject at university until I specialized in Classics. I am a great believer in direct and prolonged exposure to central texts, as against having a passing acquaintance with the contents of many texts, and I do believe that I gained from such close experience of Horace and Macaulay. At the same time, if what I have recounted so far of my 'intellectual' interests is true, it is obvious that neither Horace nor Macaulay had much appeal for me. In some ways they are, as it happens, of like feather (although I much prefer Horace), and it must have been the ascetic impulse that kept me working on them. My emotional and literary interests were more satisfied with English poetry, represented for me then, as for many of my generation, by Palgrave's *Golden Treasury*, and especially the fourth book, which ends, save for Shelley's nostalgic 'Music, when soft voices die', with Wordsworth's 'Ode on Intimations of Immortality'. This poem made a profound impression on me then. Although I had been reading

Greek more than any subject other than Latin, the fare presented to me was without any Plato. Wordsworth's poem, however, was interpreted for me by a sympathetic teacher against its philosophic, Platonic background. If the truth be told the poem does not rise to the full beauty and depth of the theme. But it was the first treatment of Platonic metaphysics that had come my way. Above all it recalled to me my own earliest persuasions that I lived in a shadow world.

For me this poem appeared to indicate, in terms not strictly Christian it was true, our source and destiny. I cannot say that I ever *believed* in Platonism. Instinctively I felt that there was no compelling rational explanation of reality; but it was a literary-philosophical quasi-explanation which one entertained *als ob*, as if it were true. It was something like the *verisimile*, the 'probable' of the New Academics, who were persuaded that the truth could never be known, but who, to avoid cessation of living, had to have recourse to what they judged to be like the truth (although how they could recognize what was like the truth, when they couldn't perceive the truth, they naturally could not explain). Nevertheless Platonism for good or evil was a potent inspiration in my life and my mind has been continuously occupied with its high thinking. So readily did these ideas in Wordsworth's poem occur to my mind that I began to see them everywhere.

Day after day a poem from Palgrave, or several stanzas of one, had to be memorized and repeated in class. Often last-minute frenzied endeavour to get this task done was irksome, if also exciting. Those concentrated efforts developed in an uncanny way one's ability to memorize, and so to enjoy, also subconsciously, a body of literature. What patterns of thought, what patterns of style, what stimulus to self-discipline, what development of the sensibility resulted from this use of memory must be significant, even if never to be assessed.

But I would not wish it to be thought that rationality is the specific, conscious work of poetry, especially in youth. Poetry is incantatory, not discursive. Few, if any, of us live a mainly rational existence: we live, being in some society, by myths, which some question more and some less. But the individual can escape.

Another preoccupation was music – not singing, which gave me great emotional satisfaction later; but, since I was the only possible pianist in the school and an accompanist was necessary for Gilbert and Sullivan, the piano. Here, although my teacher was enthusiastic (she was called 'Breezy'), I did not get anything like the skilled instruction and adequate practice that are indispensable for satisfactory performance. When I presented myself for examination in the sixth grade of the Royal Irish Academy of Music, the examiner had reservations about my interpretation and technical execution of the 'Prelude' of York Bowen's 'Suite Mignonne' (as who might not have), even if he gave me the near universal honours. Later I was to have reservations myself about the Academy's own accomplishments. Dublin, much less Ballinasloe, could hardly hope to rival Paris and Nadia Boulanger. My playing of the piano was then to be interrupted for eleven years while I was a Jesuit seminarian. It never recovered. Now I play nursery rhymes for my grandchildren with their energetic but wayward participation, a not unjoyous or useless occupation.

Soon came the end of school-days and, for the moment, scholastic effort. My last week in Garbally left me in an exhausted state, from excessive dieting and training in athletics, and with German measles during my examinations. During the long summer holidays I continued with the absurd pious routine of school, but also savoured again the delights of riding and fishing. A neighbour and friend trained hunters for sale and was happy to have his horses ridden regularly. There are few sensations more satisfying than to have a horse between one's knees put down his head and reach out for a full gallop: going into low-sounding overdrive on a high-powered car is but mildly reminiscent of it. Riding high above the countryside, especially when the whitethorn and furze were in riotous bloom and fragrant, with a distant prospect of Slieve Bloom or Slieve Aughty, was especially intoxicating. The pleasure was for me in some ways the savouring of a delight away from men. It was a communing with Nature, meaning not discourse with Nature but the sense of identification with her.

Fishing gives a very special kind of pleasure. I recollect days on Lough Atorick near Woodford with our local curate, who had been formerly a Latin master at Garbally, where he was nicknamed 'Dido'. I assume that it was his sympathy for Virgil's portrayal of the Carthaginian Queen rather than for any other reason that he had earned the sobriquet, even if he was a gentler soul than most of his peers. I had a car; he had an aunt in Woodford who supplied a picnic for us; and he paid for the boat and gillie. We fished smallish brown trout in that upland lake silently all day long, except for lunch, when the curate unburthened himself on occasion of his views on literature.

Medical certification and financial commitments over some years had to be made before I should present myself to the Jesuit novitiate. My entry was postponed for a month to allow me to go with my mother to Lourdes on pilgrimage. There is little that I recollect of this trip except the coffee in the hotel and the exotic fragrances of Paris, the flashing of the electric trolleys of the train as we made our way to Lourdes at night, the thunder and lightning in Lourdes itself, and the unbearable exposure of human suffering before the face of God in this Mecca for incurables. The constant spectacle of human beings calling desperately and piteously on God for delivery, with no apparent result, although it did not shake my faith, affected me. Here suffering man went to the raw ultimate of his belief in a beneficent God, but there was no response in human terms. The human dimension of faith seemed futile, even cruelly deceiving. One could, one supposed, contain this problem within theology. Still it was disturbing to actualize what is for almost all the time a slumbering faith and perceive what it really involves and what difficulty any human has in sustaining it. Ever since I have fought shy of places of pilgrimage. Partly I have distrusted my motives, as when I contemplated, for example, a visit to Lough Derg in County Donegal, a very old place of European pilgrimage, where, it was believed, there was an entrance to Hell. Was I merely curious? Was I seeking sensation? But I'm sure my main reason for eschewing such religious activity is the memory, reinforced by later experience, of how devastating it was for me at Lourdes to contemplate mangled human beings seeking with driven hope to impinge upon the divine. My experience of man's imploring the intervention of the deity I have found infinitely pathetic. It is one thing to 'believe' that we have ready access to God, indeed that we are mystically one with him; it is another to stand suffering and helpless on the very edge of the cliff of mortality and reach for the deliverer who does not answer. The livelier, it seems, one's faith, the greater its trial, which is not surprising. I found Lourdes on a later visit equally disturbing and the vision of its pleading sick unbearable.

Many years later a number of original documents concerning the apparitions at Lourdes were made available for publication for the first time by the ecclesiastical authorities concerned. They caused something of a sensation in continental magazines. A publisher friend invited my wife, Odile, and myself to summarize the new evidence, which we did in a small book entitled *Ordeal at Lourdes* (quickly known to our friends as *Odile at Lourdes*). The documents displayed in a remarkable way how, on the claimed intervention of the supernatural, the lay and ecclesiastical officers reacted, each honourably, but according to differing briefs. For each the experience was truly an ordeal. Cosy comprehensions quickly broke down: the *préfet*'s wife would no longer be permitted to hand down her low-cut dresses to her maids; the *préfet* himself would no longer be allowed to build stables, with their effluent, over the graves of dead Canons of the cathedral at Tarbes; on the other hand the *commissaire* of police became meticulous in enforcing order at the scene of the apparitions and recording everything that happened. The events at Lourdes quickly provoked a variety of human reactions. The local doctor saw the possibility of creating a spa, which would have professional and financial gains for him. Other visionaries sprang up all over the countryside and engaged in the most ridiculous practices. Throughout it all Bernadette, in spite of a background of extreme need, impressed her secular examiner by her simplicity, her good sense, and her serenity. In the end those who for duty or other reasons questioned the apparitions lost: *préfet* and *commissaire* were posted elsewhere and were reported to have died in the most frightful circumstances, which was altogether untrue.

Kneeling before the altar, where, according to the doctrine of transubstantiation, God is really present, I had often become startled at the enormity, in ordinary human terms, of such a belief. I was more or less quietened by the knowledge that faith was a profession of things imperceptible. To that belief, then, I had become inured. The experience of Lourdes, however, startled me much more. It was no longer merely personal: it was the experience of suffering humanity and its cry was desperate, insistent and, on the face of it, of almost no avail.

The practice of belief, however, prevailed and, like everyone else, I prayed before the grotto with outstretched hands. As the homeward train drew up out of the valley at night-time and its pilgrims sang the hymn of Lourdes and later said the Rosary, I suppose that I joined in and shared their regret on departure. What I do recollect is a girl singing a familiar aria from the *Cavalleria Rusticana*, the concluding bars of which build up to a final soaring note. Before me lay a new life beckoning.

THREE

The Youth, who daily farther from the east
Must travel, still is Nature's Priest,
And by the vision splendid
Is on his way attended.

EARLY in October 1933 I became a Jesuit postulant (for about
a fortnight) and then novice for two years at Emo Court in
Laois, designed by James Gandon for the Earl of Portarlington,
and built in the last decade of the eighteenth century. The
Government had by now afforested most of the estate, but the
elegant house with its dome, serpentine bachelor wing, and
classical portico was beautifully set beside an arboretum
looking over an artificial lake. Classical statues of such as the
huntress Diana were judiciously placed against pine trees in
peaty land, rich in rhododendrons and wild, heavily scented,
yellow azaleas in the spring. The house faced south along an
impressive avenue of Wellingtonian pines towards pleasant
rolling hills that ended with the dramatic ruined stronghold of
the O'Mores, the Rock of Dunamase.

The interior of the house was, as is usual in such houses,
good in parts. The hall floor was inlaid and there were several
rooms with fine plaster-work; but the glory of the house was
the dome, which now served as the chancel of the oratory.
There an altar had been placed, with unfortunate consequences
for the beautiful floor. An opening from the dome wall had been
made into a well-proportioned room with intricate plaster-
work on the ceiling: this served as the nave of the chapel and
gave a view northwards over ornamental gardens, containing an
avenue of sculpted Irish yews, towards the lake. Emo was much

the most pleasant and elegant of all the houses I have lived in. The Jesuits have departed, but an ex-stockbroker acquaintance now owns it and has given himself great pains to restore it to its non-institutional glory and to enable the public to see the arboretum and 'clochar' ('convent'), where shrubs are grown.

The period of postulancy was spent mainly in walks through the countryside. There were six of us, eventually to join the main group of sixteen or so who had preceded. Each of us was called an 'anima' (a soul) and every two of us were introduced to the novitiate life by an 'angelus'. Each group of three occupied a separate room known as a 'camerata'. My angelus, who had poetic leanings, explained the rules and routine of the novitiate to us with admirable detachment and subtle humour. He took a childlike pleasure in borrowing my watch (as a full novice he had surrendered his own) to monitor our progress when he and we examined our consciences for precisely a quarter of an hour twice a day. He proposed themes for meditation to us, and took what seemed like a literary and sensuous, but also spiritual, delight in conjuring up what is known as the 'composition of place', the *mise en scène*, for example, of an episode in the Gospels. His joy in the late faded flowers of the countryside in that very sunny October of 1933 made him the most delightful of companions. My introduction to the novitiate was somewhat idiosyncratic, but none the worse for that.

Soon, however, we were involved in the daily life of the novices. We were told that we would be good novices if we did nothing singular and conformed to what was *de more*, what was customary. In brief this meant getting up at 5.25 a.m.; saying the Angelus; praying; Mass; reading spiritual books and receiving spiritual instruction as the main occupation of the day; some manual work indoor and outdoor; and meals and recreation which was passed in groups of three. There was no conversation within the house, although necessary communication was allowed in Latin. We retired to bed at about half past nine. We took walks in the flat countryside once a week, sheltering from wind or rain in some ruined house or castle. We had a holiday at home in each of the two years of the novitiate: this meant fancier meals, and all-day recreation and some access to music.

Not on the face of it a very exciting regime. But all the beauty was on the inside. Our lives were animated by the ideals of Ignatius of Loyola (1491-1556), a Spanish nobleman who, being 'converted', formed a band of élite 'soldiers' of Christ – the Company or Society of Jesus. Some idea of the uncompromising obedience of this saint to the Church may be gleaned from some of his sayings:

We should so conform to the Catholic Church that, if a thing that appears to our eyes to be white is defined by her as black, we should likewise pronounce it to be black.

They who obey in will only, while their reason resists, have only one foot in religion.

'I will' and 'I won't' don't exist in our house.

We must insist more determinedly on taming the interior man than the body, and breaking the movements of our mind than the bones of our body.

Vince teipsum – conquer yourself.

The Jesuits profess an especial practice of obedience, and indeed the inner grade of their priests (for there is an élite within an élite) take not only the three solemn vows of poverty, chastity and obedience but a separate and additional vow of obedience to the Pope and also other simple vows for good measure. In Ignatius' vivid phrase, they have 'one foot in the air' in their readiness to obey. It is ironic, then, that the Society was suppressed in the eighteenth century by the Pope for many years and, more recently, appears to have encountered some papal suspicion. But, of course, the Jesuits for all their Founder's words do not give up the use of reason and, indeed, have a reputation in some quarters for intelligence and humanity.

Jesuit spirituality is related to the famous *Spiritual Exercises*, drawn up by Ignatius and used widely throughout the Catholic world in spiritual 'retreats' of eight days or less. Jesuits themselves, however, take in addition to an annual retreat of eight days the full course of these exercises, that is over a period of thirty days. This is prescribed at the beginning of their novitiate and during their 'tertianship', a further wholly spiritual year that occurs after they have become priests at the age of about thirty-three years or so.

The first 'week' of the exercises sets out from the basic proposition that man is created for God and all other things are created to help man towards this end. Man should use things, then, such as health or sickness, riches or poverty, honour or ignominy, indifferently in accordance as they help or hinder him towards his end. The ideal of detachment from and indifference to human things is a strong mark of the true Jesuit. The topics considered intensively in this first week are the sin of the angels, the sin of our first parents and our own particular sins, to which is joined an imagination of Hell through the experience of our five senses. Pretty fundamentalist stuff.

The second week begins with an imagination of the Kingdom of Christ in which Christ is seen as it were as an earthly king summoning his subjects to war: they are to share his labours, as his victories. Not to respond to this summons is to be a 'perverse knight'. Some will wish to distinguish themselves in Christ's service. There follow meditations on the Incarnation and birth of Christ, as far as possible applying all the senses and imagination to various episodes of Christ's life up to the Passion. Interspersed with these are special meditations on, for example, the 'Two Standards', the (military) standard of Christ and that of Lucifer. Here there is a lively suggestion of the activities of innumerable devils throughout the world. The followers of Christ elect for poverty in preference to riches, contempt in preference to worldly honour, and humility in preference to pride. Then there are the 'Three Divisions of Men', the first of which has a mere velleity to rid itself of an encumbrance in the service of God; the second wills to do so but does not do so effectively; and the third wills and does. Then come the Three Modes of Humility and the Three Modes of Making a Good Election, that is, the choice of one's way of life.

The third week is occupied with meditation on Christ's Passion, a harrowing experience prolonged over some four intense days. The fourth week deals with Christ's Resurrection. The exercises end with the Contemplation to excite Spiritual Love in us. Ignatius characteristically begins this by insisting that love is to be related to deeds rather than words and that it consists in an exchange of what they have between lover and loved one. For God's many gifts to me, I should make return. God dwells in all existing things, in things vegetative, sensible and intellectual and so in all of me. I am his temple, the image of his divine majesty. God works for me in all creatures. All goods and gifts descend from his infinite potency to me. What am I to do in return? To the *Exercises* are appended the Three Modes of Praying. The first of these is the examination of one's performance in relation to the ten commandments, the seven deadly sins, the three powers of the soul and the five senses of the body; the second is the consideration of each word of, for example, the 'Lord's Prayer' or the 'Ave Maria' and so on; the third is to consider each such word for the length of a breath, concentrating on the meaning of the word, or the person to whom it is addressed, or one's own vileness.

There is a spareness about these *Exercises* when summarized thus that would for most people be distinctly rebarbative. They reflect, of course, their times and their composer's earlier profession of obedience in arms. They give prominence to no subtle or exalted theology. On the other hand they engage all of the senses, and not only the intellect, in savouring the

purport of any theme. There is not only intense consideration
of these themes, but repetition, and again repetition, of these
considerations. Clarity of purpose in every exercise is insisted
upon. The retreatant must pursue relentlessly that which he
seeks, the *id quod volo*. Absolute submission to the King, absolute self-discipline, absolute detachment from things, indeed a
preference to serve in the harder way, so as to prove one's
loyalty and love. *Ad maiorem Dei gloriam*, 'To the greater glory
of God': that is the battle-cry of Ignatius and the Jesuits.

The *Exercises* are meant to be directed and, to have their full
and proper effect, must last four weeks. In this way they
become, in the more sombre parts, starker, it is true; but also
they are amplified, and the lessons of Jesus in the Gospels
occupy by far most of the time. Here the Director, in
accordance with Ignatius' own instructions, can explore different levels and methods of theology, culminating, as do the
Exercises themselves, in the contemplation of love. It is clear
from Ignatius' instructions on the discernment of spirits that he
presumes the subject will experience consolation, even to tears,
and rapture as well as (and more likely, perhaps) desolation of
the spirit. The Director is to help with everything.

I underwent the experience of the *Exercises* in the month
before Christmas in 1933. The weather was for most of the time
unusually cold and frosty. Hour by hour and day by day we
walked up and down the avenue of Irish yews reflecting, as the
technical and curious phrase went, 'on the interior outside'. We
were walking outside, but we were reviewing what we had
meditated on within ourselves: Ignatius made doubly sure we
got everything to sink in. The light over towards Diana across
the lake on her promontory underneath the pines was bewitching. One or two of the 'monks' (Jesuits *are* technically monks,
but the Jesuits use the term somewhat jocosely of themselves)
now and again responded to one another's occasional halloos
over the echoing lake. Such skittish outbreaks occurred, but

very occasionally, through too much tension. During short periods of manual labour we had vast quantities of leaves to rake and laurels to cut back in the arboretum. Here the brown against the darker raked earth afforded an autumnal satisfaction. Then it was all over on Christmas Eve.

The Master of novices who directed the *Exercises* for us was a kindly man with eyes that blinked solemnly, or again smilingly, behind his small, steel spectacles. He was middle-aged, pale and delicate, slim, with cropped grey hair and a slightly mincing gait. He had been on the missions in China and was initially merely filling in for the official Master who had what was inelegantly termed a 'broken head', some kind of spiritual or mental exhaustion resulting in an inability to concentrate. The cure for a broken head was to be put, in another surprising image, 'out to grass'. The treatment of good feeding, good sleeping and little mental work appeared to be mostly successful. But a few sad men spent all of their lives more or less on pasture. In due course our temporary novice-master became permanent. In some ways he was cut out for the job.

Although by non-novices he was known as 'Pa', he had qualities that suggested that he should rather have been called 'Ma', for he was somewhat motherly. Piety sat on him easily, which made his office of spiritual instruction and example in asceticism easier for him to sustain for many years in middle life than it would have been for many more robust types. He had a love of nature and a love of poetry including some favourite contemporary poems, from both of which we profited. He seized many occasions to bring us out into the fields to identify wild flowers, collect wild strawberries in the woods, or spot the various birds, including (appropriately) a colony of squawking blue Jays that inhabited the arboretum. He had a weakness for excursions, and was happiest walking along through narrow muddy or leafy lanes by the commissariat cart talking quietly of his experiences in China, Macao and Hong Kong. Even his more formal instructions on the *Constitution* of the Jesuits were laced with verse or anecdote, the latter usually announcing itself irrepressibly well in advance with a bright twinkle of his rather beady eye. In such ways he lightened the spareness of asceticism.

For all his gentle qualities he was adventurous and courageous too. As we were mere beginners in the spiritual life, needing (God help us) to be purged of worldliness and apprenticed solidly and comprehensively in Jesuit spirituality, he was not encouraged to take us with him on flights into the higher regions. We heard little indeed of the quietism of Caussade's *Abandonment to the Divine Providence* or Lallement's true doctrine, or the higher speculations of the near-contemporaries Rousselot or Maréchal, all Jesuits though they were. Still he did measure out to us carefully the doctrine (and practice) of the mystical body which was growing in popularity at the time. This is an intoxicating potion, for it teaches literally that each one of us is one with, or rather is, Christ, who, of course, is God. He is the vine, we are the branches. I well remember the excitement that a particular, and particularly turgid, book called *Christ the Life of the Soul*, written by Abbot Marmion of Maredsous (educated by the Jesuits in Dublin), provoked in me as I meditated upon its teachings on this matter. This kind of meditation was sustained during all conscious hours by recalling the doctrine as often as possible (and so 'realizing' it), and recording how often, on little beads made up of units and tens, pinned inside one's gown. The number on this was transferred to a special little notebook at the quarter-hour examination of one's conscience twice a day.

This welcomed indoctrination, it must be remembered, was conducted in an almost total absence of other influences. We had access to no books other than selected spiritual ones, no newspapers, no radio, no cinema, no music, other than our own singing of Gregorian chant and hymns. We went outside only once a week and always with two companions. We were not allowed to meet members of the community other than the Master of novices and his assistant, known as the Socius, except on special feast-days, when limited 'fusion' was allowed. We spoke no English in the house and our hours for conversation outside were restricted, were conducted in groups of three, included a period of conversation in Latin, and excluded quite a number of 'forbidden' topics considered, most of them sensibly, as inappropriate or simply, as in the case of food or money, bad form.

Such a regime freely embraced, naturally provided optimum conditions for much acquaintance with, if not actual progress in, the spiritual life. The absence of all distraction greatly provided for concentration on spiritual things. One was buoyed up with the overwhelming thought of Christ's sacrifice in the Mass (so marvellously described by de la Taille's *Mysterium Fidei*), Christ's real presence in the Eucharist, Christ's mystical presence in oneself. One was an 'alter Christus', another Christ, as was every other man. Our effort was to let Christ take over, so to speak, in us and ourselves to retreat in our insignificance. The ideal was that of John the Baptist who, speaking of Christ, whose precursor he was, declared that he himself should diminish, as Christ increased: *illum oportet crescere, me autem minui*. It was impossible not to feel at times that this indwelling of Christ in one was too flattering to human nature; but one either believed this or was confused, and all the pressures were towards belief. The Epistle of Trinity Sunday is in awe of what God can do: 'O the depth of the riches of the wisdom and of the knowledge of God! How incomprehensible are his judgements, and how unsearchable his ways! For who hath known the mind of the Lord?' How could one question? Christ had conquered totally. The eroticism of passages from the *Song of Solomon* was instinctively sublimated and had no other object than Christ. One did not dwell too long on such passages, not because of their potentially perilous sensuousness, but because one could not honestly aspire to the implied mysticism. But they could symbolize modest aspirations towards union with Christ (a usual formula) that were regarded as desirable. They marked also a sustained level of intense spiritual effort and preoccupation. They constituted a long-continuing vision of 'reality'.

As for other eroticism, it was kept very much at bay by our whole manner of life and other-worldly preoccupations. It is doubtful if our practice of mortification in itself contributed much to its control. We knelt on and kissed the floor of the refectory before the assembled community and with out-stretched hands proclaimed our 'fault' (perhaps not keeping our eyes cast down modestly). We kissed the shoes of our brothers as they sat at dinner to humiliate ourselves. We took meals on our knees for some fault of greater 'gravity', a diverting, if also a little embarrassing, experience. We knelt before all the novices in the quarter of charity and had them criticize, some of them with what seemed insufficiently concealed minor malice, our shortcomings. On rising in the morning we commonly washed our whole bodies with a linen towel soaked in cold water, even in winter. We wore a light chain about our wrist with many sharp spikes digging, but harmlessly, into our flesh: this was really painful only when one bumped against someone or something. We did this only for a few hours a day about twice a week. We lashed our backs with the discipline, a rough, knotted cat-o'-nine-tails, during the time it took to recite aloud that interminable and fearful Psalm, the Miserere. We did this normally at bedtime, again about twice a week. I can easily remember my human recoil from this flogging when it was signalled by a wretched bell, the tintinnabulum. My back never bore scars such as were seen on some of the others when they went to swim. Such mortification is trifling. What is difficult about it is its self-infliction, because it goes so much against one's instincts. For this reason, although I engaged in it conscientiously, I found it somewhat degrading. If according to Christian teaching our bodies are honoured in being temples of the Holy Spirit, in the Word taking our flesh, and in that flesh being resurrected, one would think that Christianity would have escaped more from the bewitching charms of Platonism which dishonours the body absolutely. Plotinus was ashamed of being in a body. This conflict of view on the body was the great point of issue between Augustine and the dominant Neoplatonist, Porphyry, at the most vital period in the evolution of the Christian West. But although the Neoplatonists appeared to lose, once again *Graecia capta ferum victorem cepit*: 'captured Greece captured her fierce conqueror'. Much of what passes for specifically Christian teaching in practice comes to us almost directly from the world of Greece and Rome.

Mortification caused me little anxiety. Meals rather more. The conspiring of everybody to eat what was 'of custom', and the pattern of meals which had been traditional in the squirearchy of the nineteenth century and was imitated perforce by Catholics who wanted to keep their side up, and our youthful undistracted appetites, all made for conspicuous consumption. This was most in evidence at the main meal of the day which took place at three or four o'clock. Plentiful soup was followed by two generous courses of meat, vegetables and potatoes, themselves followed by an optional dish of mutton passed around, this followed by copious dessert. On feast-days, which happened on average two or three days in the week, dinner was followed by coffee, cake, fruit and sweets, the contents of parcels sent by parents, now shared equally by all. My frequently distended stomach provoked the thought that it would not live up to my vocation. Small wonder that when we then repaired to the chapel for half an hour's meditation, many drowsy heads bobbed up and down. In these unhappy, happy circumstances the drill was that the victim stood up to fend off the embrace of dreamy-eyed sleep. But sometimes he would soon begin to sway dangerously, causing pleasant anxiety to his brethren. Tittering might ensue which, since we observed so much silence and had not altogether lost our animal spirits, ended in the hysterical laughter of some and the constrained merriment of others.

Not being 'singular' and conforming to what was customary extended to many areas of our lives, our speech, for example. There is nothing like reciting aloud together the same prayers day after day for years to induce in youths, especially if they have 'a good ear', a great conformity in pronunciation. In addition we practised the same exercises in voice production and breath control every morning, ignoring one another, in the shrubbery. Every now and then we preached the same set and very rhetorical sermon, called 'the ordinary tone', with appropriate studied gestures before the Socius and our colleagues for their predictable criticisms. During May each of us inflicted a *ferverino* on the Blessed Virgin on our brothers as they divided their attention between our eloquence and their supper. During dinner the Master of novices corrected us on phrasing or pronunciation ('whol-ly, brother', 'articulate the consonants') when our duty was from time to time to read some improving, not necessarily pious, but carefully censored book. We would have rehearsed our reading beforehand with a colleague who was considered better at reading in public. Nothing much was left to chance.

It was at this time that I was encouraged in a modest way in developing my voice. The Socius, a tall handsome man who had lived in Australia for some time, was himself interested in singing and professed to find my voice worthy of attention. He prepared me for various solos in the chapel, and sometimes in a neighbouring parish church on feast-days, and a soirée or two at Christmas. My repertoire consisted of the usual pious tenor songs: 'Panis Angelicus', Schubert's and Gounod's 'Ave Marias', Gounod's 'Ave Verum'. But there was an interesting 'Pater Noster' and especially an 'Ave Maria' by Fauré which I greatly liked. Singing in choir and the Gregorian chant allowed suitable emotional expression to a life singularly simple and intense.

Conformation extended even to our bodily repose and movement. The *Rules of Modesty* prescribed that we held our heads straight, slightly bending downward; that we kept our eyes still and cast down, and that we looked not at the eyes of others, but below them, especially if they exercised authority; and that we kept our hands quiet and our gait unhurried.

How successful all this effort towards conformation in mind and body was, I cannot say. But I do think that it did leave a strong impression on all of us, and a sense of union and unity of high spiritual purpose that made for a great loyalty to one another in the Company of Jesus. We were deeply committed to the purpose of the Society which was the salvation of one's neighbour, itself to be the proper means towards our own salvation.

Little of external importance happened to me over these two years. I got rheumatic fever and was well cared for. I took part in the usual 'experiments' – washing pots and pans for a month in the kitchen and visiting the patients in the local workhouse. A red-letter day, by novitiate standards, was one on which one arrived (without skipping what went before) at the chapters in the prescribed reading of Rodriguez' *Christian Doctrine*, 'in which preceding doctrine' – comprehensive, sound, and heavy – 'is confirmed by examples'. Then one could lean back in one's chair and give oneself up to the delights of reading for the umpteenth time about Simon Styletes, and Paphnucius the Abbot, and the other diverting denizens of the *Spiritual Meadow*. The stories of our remote precursors in the spiritual combat were highly entertaining.

It will doubtless have been gathered from these pages that Christ was truly master of the soul of a novice in the Society of Jesus. I probably have failed to conjure up for worldly eyes anything of the 'vision splendid' which sustained us. It was a special kind of happiness which one was fortunate to have had, even if some might judge it damaging or just a waste of time.

The novitiate ended with the taking of the three simple vows of religion, whereby one became formally a Jesuit, without however taking any order or direct commitment to the priesthood. In my time indeed one still heard of Jesuit scholastics, as we were now called, who remained so for all their lives. One discarded one's lay clothes and dressed in dog-collar and clericals – and recovered one's watch. My last memories of my final days as a regular dweller in Emo was of the profusion of asters in the dewy September beds.

FOUR

At length the Man perceives it die away,
And fade into the light of common day.

MY NEXT ABODE, while I was to attend university studies in Dublin, was Rathfarnham Castle, situated in the south-western suburbs of the city. The castle had been built towards the close of the sixteenth century by Archbishop Loftus and had later been owned by William Conolly, Speaker of the Irish House of Commons. Its unsuccessful entrance arch, now removed, was built in the early nineteenth century by Lord Ely, who sold his vote for the Union with England in 1800 for £45,000. The castle had been intended as a fortress between Dublin and the mountains and was used for military purposes in 1641 and later. It is impressive but hardly beautiful. The additions of a retreat house and study house, where I lived, made by the Jesuits during their occupancy, now ended, added no distinction.

The grounds were fairly extensive, looking towards a golfcourse and the Dublin mountains, and were well wooded on the side of the house of studies. There a river, with a small turbine for electricity, provided an artificial lake dominated by bedraggled-looking Muscovite ducks. There was also a small aviary which lit up a corner of the wood. It was a pleasant place and gave the feeling of being above and outside of the city.

Although I spent four years in Rathfarnham Castle I saw little of its grand rooms other than the one along the front on the first storey, which had been converted into a chapel. The castle had had ceilings painted by Angelica Kaufmann, but there had been some more innocent substitutions. When I was librarian for a short period it was my duty to lock newspapers for the priests into their sticks (which were not to be removed); this allowed me to pass through the fine hall and some other rooms and incidentally glance vaguely at the alarming newspaper headlines about the Spanish Civil War.

The air of the pre-independence period of only thirteen years before, when some English-Protestant, Dublin Castle, values affected Jesuit living, lingered here. The spiritual excesses of a politically dominating Catholicism were about to engulf the place. But an earlier, slightly 'Castle Catholic' regime still survived, mainly in the Rector. He would have been convincing as a squire, with cropped grey hair, a square red face, heavy build and ponderous movements. He had held high office and had been Provincial in charge of all Irish Jesuits and their Missions. He was confident in his ways and unimpressed by new developments, political or religious. The province in his time had shared many activities with England and there had been common training, as in, for example, the Tertianship in Wales. Englishmen such as Gerard Manley Hopkins and Father Joseph Darlington, whose contribution to Joyce's interest in style is touched on in *Stephen Hero*, were instances of the English presence. More recently Australian scholastics had lived in Rathfarnham Castle and were allowed some unusual privileges (such as the pennies to buy a newspaper, when they went out for a walk on a Sunday) on the grounds that they should get the most out of their sojourn in, what was for some of them, the old country. The Rector, then, was set in his ways, had his own ideas of how young scholastics should be so to speak debriefed from their novitiate attitudes, and quietly co-operated no more than was necessary with the then Provincial. When it suited him, he was a man of masterly inaction, few words, and rather cheerful bland countenance.

The Provincial had accepted the new way of doing things in

which the Church in Ireland was untrammelled by any restraints upon its excesses that might arise from the State. The politicians were subservient. He was a little man, fat, homely, and, understandably, unpretentious. He was seized, however, with zeal for the holy rule and was rather frustrated by the Rector of Rathfarnham Castle. On the only occasion on which I heard both of them speak to us in public, the Provincial urged a new way of doing things in one particular. The Rector thanked him and jovially shared with us the view that change had to be slow. But when the Rector's term of office was up, we were unprotected from, indeed peculiarly exposed to, the Provincial's zeal. But for my first year in the Juniorate, as it was called, all seemed well.

It was a new experience to have the use of a bicycle, even if only for going to and from University College daily and occasional more distant excursions into the Dublin and Wicklow mountains. Moreover only one companion instead of two, for mutual support, was considered necessary. Every Sunday we walked to the Pine Forest or Glencullen or Glenasmole or Upper Lough Bray. Sometimes we got as far as Lough Tay and real stalwarts walked over the Sally Gap to Glendalough and back. We usually met in groups of six or so for lunch at a rendezvous, and there boiled our billy-cans for the strongest tea I have ever seen or tasted. Some times indeed we sheltered miserably from the inexorable rain, but mostly my recollection is of sunny days, the blue firmament, and the unending expanse of purple heather. It was a wonderful liberation of the spirit, and from 'spiritual' things too. These mountains remain for me a source of continuing delight. They have become my 'home', with which on occasion I feel, though animate, as one.

During our yearly holiday or 'villa' we had the opportunity of experiencing Wordsworth's other Voice, the sea. There were some sixty of us in the Juniorate and so we needed large and inexpensive accommodation, involving little transport. Gormanston Castle, between Balbriggan and Drogheda, was ideal for our purposes. This property belonged to the Preston family since 1363 and from it they took their title of Viscounts Gormanston. They had been conspicuous as Catholic leaders until the time of Daniel O'Connell. The present handsome castle, now used by the Franciscans in conjunction with a large school, was more or less restored in 1800. It had a fine baronial hall. Beside the castle was a delightful, small seventeenth-century chapel then in poor condition. The grounds had interesting trees and shrubs, but what I remember especially was the all-pervading and sensuous smell of garlic that met one as one made one's way up the avenue. Gormanston was marvellously placed for exploring the Boyne valley and its tumuli, Monasterboice and Tara, but especially the sea, from Rush, Loughshinney and Skerries to Bettystown and Clogher Head. I have the most vivid recollections of lying back in the dunes at Bettystown, hearing and seeing the meadow pipits as they sang out their hearts against a radiant sky. Once again the sensation I had was of ease, of freedom from oppression. The oppression came, I'm sure, from anxiety about my studies but also, I believe, from the intensity of our way of life.

My daily occupation, however, was my studies, mainly in University College, Dublin. This was technically not a university: it was a Constituent College of the National University of Ireland, established in 1908, the last attempt by the English to solve the university problem in Ireland. All during the nineteenth century demand had been growing for the provision of some university education for Catholics, who in a general way were debarred (both by their Church and Trinity) from entering Trinity College, also called Dublin University. In 1845 Queen's Colleges were established at Belfast, Cork and Galway, but they were boycotted by the Catholic bishops as 'godless'. The Catholic Church then got a papal charter to found a Catholic University, which opened in Dublin in 1854, and of which it invited the recent famous convert, John Henry Newman, to be Rector. Newman's ideas on the purposes of his university, to be seen in his *Idea of a University* and elsewhere in his copious writings, were soon discovered not to be *ad unum* with those of the sponsoring bishops. He spoke of the independence of reason from faith and had his eye on forming the Catholic 'gentlemen', English as well as Irish. The bishops did not encourage these ideas, nor in due course did the Irish poor who supplied literally the pennies to pay for the university. Newman achieved much quickly and at little expense: his interesting books on university education, the acquisition of some distinguished teaching staff, the building of the unusual church, designed by John Hungerford Pollen, in St Stephen's Green, and the purchase of a whole medical school then located in Cecilia Street. Nevertheless, he soon returned to England to give himself to other things. In 1881 the Government established the Royal University of Ireland which merely examined and awarded degrees. One of the colleges which prepared students for these examinations was a continuation of the former Catholic University now known as University College, Dublin, and was entrusted to the Jesuits. It was here that Hopkins was an unhappy professor and Joyce, according to his own account, a raffish student. It was felt nevertheless that Catholics had still not got equal opportunities of university education with Protestants. Many proposals were made around the turn of the century, including the foundation of a Catholic College alongside Trinity College within Dublin University – a proposal to my mind most unfortunately defeated by die-hard groups both within Trinity and within the Catholic hierarchy. Finally, however, the National University was established in 1908 with Constituent Colleges in Galway and Cork (the old Queen's Colleges) and Dublin (the old University College). It was this College, then sited for the most part in Earlsfort Terrace, near St Stephen's Green, that I attended. It was commonly known as the 'National', reflecting both that it was, and still is, the biggest university in the country and that it drew its students from the country as a whole. Its main building, now the National Concert Hall, was designed by R. M. Butler, who had been an assistant to Sir Arthur Evans at the excavations of Knossos, and who had made his own notes on the findings at the time.

Although I took a great deal of interest in English and Irish in my first year, I concentrated mainly on Greek and Latin and read Classics through to my M. A. degree. Here the dominating professor, Michael Tierney, who came from my own part of the country and from my own school there, had had a chequered and controversial career in politics and public life and was immensely stimulating as a conversationalist and teacher. He had listened to the great Wilamowitz-Moellendorff in Berlin, and visited archaeological and other sites in Greece. He had the capacity of suggesting that he was passing on to you a message from Aeschylus or Plato or Pindar. That was why we waited patiently for him to arrive nearly half an hour late every day, and stayed on after the time class should have ended for an equal period. In between, as we sat around a long mahogany table, upon our cowering heads he showered, Aeschylus-like, large gobbets of German (especially) and French philological erudition. He wrote little and that, like his lectures, was highly stimulating if disappointingly undigested. His real interest lay in politics, active politics. He was endearingly tolerant of mystified students and of a student who continually bobbed his head in sleep within reach of his hand. He had a habit of cocking his head to one side and asking with a sympathetic chuckle and eager smile such questions as 'What does the Turkish *effendi* mean?' Some of us in due course caught on and took our turns in affording him the satisfaction of the answers expected. He was keen on Comparative Philology, Minoan Archaeology, Greek composition, accentuation and metres. We read with him Homer, Aeschylus, Sophocles, Euripides, Aristophanes, Plato and Aristotle, among other authors, and all of them seemed to be his favourites and on all of them he reported to us the views of the most recent scholars.

Later when Eduard Fraenkel allowed me to join his seminar on the *Agamemnon* of Aeschylus in Oxford, I found myself comparatively well prepared by Tierney in Dublin. He loved to recite in his pleasant accent choral odes from Sophocles' *Antigone* on the wonder of man and on love. He was passionate about the socially and politically conservative views of Aristophanes. In a small book, *Education in a Free Ireland*, published before 1922, he had proposed that education in the coming new Ireland should be free up to eighteen years of age and conducted in one type of school. Here laymen should be employed, and the parents should have more influence than the teachers, and the teachers than the priests. He vigorously attacked the notion of educating for industry or commercialism: 'We must have as our fundamental purpose the education of all Irishmen as good Irishmen and as good men, irrespective of their present economic position and with no regard for their future economic prospects.' The aim was to give 'every single citizen the education of a gentleman [shades of Newman], no longer a man of gentle birth – but of gentle mind'. One can see how his enthusiasms were generous, and suspiciously doctrinaire.

When he came to read Plato with us the books he chose were the *Euthydemus*, the *Phaedo*, the *Symposium* and the *Republic*. The metaphysical and, so to speak, mystical dimensions of these texts seized me. They were interpreted by Tierney against the background of Orphism (on which he was very keen), a mystic cult according to which man was both soul (divine) and body (evil): the soul was imprisoned in the body from which it must be freed for eventual happiness in an afterlife. Man had originated in the Titans who had eaten of the limbs of

Dionysus, the offspring of Zeus. Man, therefore, was, in a sense, God and his purpose should be to purify himself of his evil nature and release his divine. The Christian doctrine of the mystical body appeared to have at least some resemblances to this. One might account for such resemblances on the grounds that man, being constituted in a certain way, must express himself in religion, as in other matters, in the same general way. Which might be true enough, but this in turn weakens claims of exclusiveness.

Although the *Phaedo* and the *Republic* occupied most of the time I gave to Plato in my undergraduate years, the *Symposium* symbolized the highlight of my interest in him. I was not impervious to the comedy in this work, but the speech of Diotima on Love became for me, as for others before me, a basic text for reference.

What may we suppose to be the felicity of the man who sees absolute beauty in its essence, pure and unalloyed, who is able to apprehend divine beauty where it exists apart and alone? And having brought forth and nurtured true goodness he will have the privilege of being beloved of God, and becoming, if ever a man can, immortal himself. This absolute beauty, *suddenly* revealed to him at the end of his initiation, is a beauty existing alone in itself, unique, eternal, and all other beautiful things partake of it, yet in such manner that, while they come into being and pass away, it neither undergoes any increase or diminution nor suffers any change.

(Translated by Walter Hamilton)

Sappho, Rousseau, Dante, and so many others, have described how they were overcome by some love, physical or mental or, to do more justice to man, a union of both: *ecce deus fortior me qui veniens dominabitur mihi.* 'Behold a god, stronger than me, who coming, will be my master.' So wrote Dante in his *Vita Nuova.* The Platonic ascent has ever beckoned on, ennobling, deluding, refining, dehumanizing. It marries well with an easy Christianity, compensating for the latter's failure in practice to live among the heights, and being compensated by Christ's compassion for poor and suffering humanity.

Be that as it may, Tierney on occasions quoted Plotinus also with enthusiasm at our little group:

. . . passing, on the upward way, all that is other than God, each in the solitude of himself shall behold that solitary-dwelling Existence, the Apart, the Unmingled, the Pure, that from Which all things depend, for Which all look and live and act and know, the Source of Life and Intellection and of Being.

And one that shall know this vision – with what passion of love shall he not be seized, with what pang of desire, what longing to be molten into one with This, what wondering delight!

(Translated by Stephen MacKenna)

The passage comes from *Ennead* I.6, 'On Beauty', a famous essay and one that we know, confidently, affected Augustine. Tierney rolled off the Greek text with obvious relish. What I knew then of his political career and what I know of his later career as President of University College, Dublin, does not suggest much sensitivity or aestheticism in him. But being sensitive and being doctrinaire are not incompatible. We are in the land of extremes, on the road of excess, said to be bound for the palace of Wisdom.

These Platonic and Neoplatonic enthusiasms – for they were little more – were responsible for my interest since then in the Irish philosopher of the ninth century, Johannes Scottus Eriugena, now referred to more conveniently as Eriugena. Here was a man, writing in Latin, who, having a knowledge of the Greek language altogether remarkable in the West in the ninth century, sought to reconcile the dominating somewhat de-Platonized Augustinianism of the West with the Neoplatonized theology of the Greek Fathers: of Dionysius the Areopagite, Maximus the Confessor and Gregory of Nyssa, among others. His great work on the *Division of Nature* had been misunderstood and neglected. There was no good modern edition of its text, no commentaries, and no translation into any modern language except an indifferent one into German made towards the end of the nineteenth century. Would it not be worthwhile to undertake to study him and perhaps even repair some of the neglect? So it was that I was later to propose for a doctorate thesis in Oxford the topic 'Prolegomena to the *Contra Academicos* of St Augustine', which allowed me to explore Augustine on the one hand and Plotinus and his disciple Porphyry on the other.

It is, I think, wrong to assume that such long commitments hold continuing interest and delight for those that embrace them. It is not my experience. There are reaches of Augustine, the Neoplatonists, and Eriugena that fail to appeal to me. There are other pursuits in life that strongly call to me. Yet one goes on, partly perhaps for reasons of *history*: to make known the truth, however little more, about some important figure in the past; to remove from him the imputations, favourable or unfavourable, which successful groups in bolstering their power, in good faith or confusedly or in simple bad faith, attribute to him. This, however small an achievement in itself, participates in the transcending importance of the discovery of truth, which is ultimately one. If the figures one is seeking to present anew are important in history, in the history of ideas, then the motivation is more easily understood. But still a residue remains of some overriding attraction to the intellectual dimension and quality of the ideas that aroused one's interest in the first place. The human mind can have many affinities, but one of them especially may tend to have its way.

The professor of Latin in University College was a shy Victorian who sported a winged collar under a round ruddy face that appeared apoplectic at times through force of assumed anger. Then indignation whistled in his teeth. We knew it was a show of strength where there was excessive mildness. He blushed uneasily and hurried on whenever, which is often in Latin literature, one came upon an indelicate word or passage. I cannot now recall if or how he handled the Attis poem in

Catullus; but it was a poem that much disturbed me. It starts at a rattling frenetic pace and immediately describes how on Phrygian soil Attis, an aspiring Greek disciple of the wild goddess Cybele, hacks off his genitals with a sharp stone in hatred of love. He and his companions, now referred to for the most part as female, give themselves to an orgiastic rout, but eventually fall asleep through exhaustion. In the pale light of morning she, Attis, realizing what she has done, rushes desperately to the sea-shore and, facing Greece, her civilized homeland, laments her fate. Cybele sends a lion to drive her into the forests, there to live out her life in obedience to her vow. Catullus turns aside in the last three lines of the poem to pray that such madness may pass him by.

There are a few scholars who see in this poem evidence of a (surprisingly) mystical tendency in Catullus. Others see in it a protest against the castrating effect on him of his relations with Lesbia. When I read it first, I recognized with some horror that it might have relevance for those who had made themselves eunuchs for Christ's sake. More disturbing, however, were details of the cult of Attis which I found in the ordinary way in Ellis's commentary on the poem: the celebration of the death and 'resurrection' of Attis bore striking resemblances to the ceremonies of Holy Week celebrating the death and resurrection of Christ – even to the inclusion of a tree, the way of the cross. Comparative religion, I again felt, dealing with the same human nature, weakens exclusive claims.

The simpler, more erotic, themes of Catullus, greatly restricted in the Victorian school selection used by the professor, had little effect upon me. Our ideals and way of life were an incredibly efficient insulation. Women in the flesh created no problem. Those we saw were mostly nuns who, presumably on instruction from less liberal superiors than ours, to avoid distraction occupied all the front seats in the classroom, a sea of black, entirely featureless. One gorgeous girl did attract our attention. She was the only girl reading Ancient History. The class was held in a small museum, full of dark show-cases, around a dull black table. She always arrived late bringing with her confused apologies, a bright dress, and a whiff of perfume. From the consideration of the horny hands of the lecturer, gesturing over the gloomy table, we were amused to glance at his pale blue smiling eyes as they welcomed this expected and late intrusion. She was Darina Laracy, later my friend and the wife of Ignazio Silone.

Meanwhile there had been a change of regime at Rathfarnham Castle. A new Rector and a new Prefect of Studies had been installed to give effect to the 'reforming' of the Provincial. The Prefect of Studies was a small man, well intentioned, not evidently stupid, but definitely without much sense: 'the villainies of the virtuous, who shall recount them' – so wrote Norman Douglas in *Alone*. This minor superior supervised our going out to University College and our coming home. We had instructions from him to take certain specified routes which he patrolled from time to time. He checked out our desks in our absence. He asked searching questions, and was always entering something copiously, with a sick and harassed smile, in a small notebook. He was a tired but eager and programmed agent, who doubtless was being, as he saw it, merely obedient.

Some of the young men spoke among themselves of this priest, and of the rather simple-minded Rector, and of the unimaginative Provincial. Their innocent enough and at worst jocose reactions to a 'reformation' for which there was no need were reported, perhaps on inquisition, back to the superiors. For the Jesuits have a diabolical rule which says that if any of them gets to know of a 'grave temptation' that besets another, he should warn the superior of it. Criticizing the Superior, in whom one is instructed to see the Lord, Christ, can seem to the tiro a grave fault in another. Moreover the *Constitution* of the

Society imposes on its members acceptance that any thing whatever that is noticed in them may be reported by anyone, except a Confessor, to superiors. They should be prepared to split on one another mutually, especially when questioned by the Superior. Fortunately Jesuits of even a few years' experience of the Society use common sense in relation to such prescriptions. But in these instances around 1936 in Rathfarnham Castle modest enough peccadilloes were reported to superiors who, through misplaced zeal for good, exaggerated them dramatically. A number of scholastics had ecclesiastical sanctions read over them (a very grave and rare occurrence) as they knelt before all in the refectory; a few were ordered to repeat the thirty days' retreat of their noviceship; and two quite innocent bystanders, so to speak, broke under the tension of the affair as it climaxed, and had to repair to a mental institution. The damage done interiorly to many cannot be measured. The whole episode was petty but also, unfortunately, tragic: for the service of these young men was idealistic and voluntary and their lives by any normal standard exemplary.

I was bemused by the affair and could never understand why superiors should take such extravagant action for trifles, reported by those whose early zeal was insufficiently tempered by common sense. I was deeply disturbed. I had been reading in Lucretius how Agamemnon willed the slaughter of his innocent daughter Iphianassa in the name of 'religion': *tantum religio potuit suadere malorum*. The cases were not the same, but the following of Christ on which I had embarked had revealed itself to me as not without its danger.

Soon, what with this sad deception, the growing problems created for me by the attractions of Platonism, and the evidences afforded by comparative religion, I was reduced to a sorely troubled state. *The* singing-master of my soul appeared to lose authority. I was tempted to curse the God whose yoke I had so eagerly welcomed. The Spiritual Father had no help to offer. This, he said, was normal. His words were few. His embarrassment was great. He stalled on every question. He resorted to whistling. Truly, he had emptied himself for Christ. But I took his assurance, without being assured, as right. For me he spoke as Christ: I believed this, however uneasily, or I believed nothing. That was what was insidious about the whole situation. Your superiors decided for you. You had no will of your own. The Superior's will and judgment were to be the rule for your will and judgment. This is what the *Constitution* of the Society imposes.

So the months dragged on. I was too enamoured of the life as a whole, its ideals, and the friendship of good companions to want to change. In *The Young Augustine* I have written of 'those who have tasted the joys of an intellectual life lived in the close companionship of friends, all bent on the same ultimate goal, all contributing in some way to the delight of discovery, all responsive to a feeling of sympathy and affection'. I had experienced this. And so I continued to 'believe' what I was told to believe, that I would in due course emerge into calmer waters. The 'dark night of the soul' referred indeed to mystical experiences, but it also referred to the aridity and near despair of an ordinary experience. This was how faith was tested. Even St Peter denied the Lord.

Life, moreover, was very full and, though by no means soft, agreeable. My work was challenging. Apart from Classics, with its wide range of attendant interests, such as vase-painting (the Classics' museum had a fine collection of vases), and comparative philology, I took up Hebrew and had some exposure to Sanskrit and linguistics. I got most emotional satisfaction, however, from singing. There was a good choir in the Jesuit theologate not far away, which was often invited to broadcast, especially at Christmas and Holy Week. Its conductor invited me to join them on these occasions and at the funerals of Jesuits in the main Jesuit church in Dublin. I shall never forget my first

five minutes practising with this choir. I was placed between
two mature and excellent tenors. Previous experience had led
me to believe that I could sing. In this new situation I couldn't
hear myself. I soon discovered what resonance is. We sang
mostly polyphony, motets of Palestrina and Vittoria. Solo-
singing can be an almost intoxicating experience, but singing in
a choir gives participation in a greater range of harmony which
can be overpowering. Many of the liturgical chants in Latin
speak most eloquently to the human heart, not least some of
those that commit poor humans to the grave. Then the comfort
of community reaches deepest. *Et tu puer, filius Altissimi
vocaberis.*

At the end of the month in which the Second World War
broke out I had completed my M. A. degree and won a
travelling studentship in Classics. I should then normally have
gone to a foreign university, probably Berlin or Leipzig, to
pursue classical studies. As it was, my use of the studentship
was postponed, and I was sent instead to what was known as
the 'Bog', the Jesuit philosophate near Tullamore, in the great
central bowl of Ireland. I welcomed this, mostly because, unlike
in the university where each of us studied different groups of
subjects, we would, as in the novitiate, all be doing the same
courses together. *Cor unum et anima una.* My mental and spiritual condition yearned for this. Besides, scholastic philosophy,
which was intended to supply rational underpinning to
Christian theology, would surely help me in my difficulties. I
looked forward too to a more leisurely pace of life, simpler and
rural surroundings, the wind-swept bogs, the clean air and,
especially, the open sky. To hear and gaze up at the wild geese
flying V-shaped from horizon to horizon against a sky lit red at
evening – what prospect could have been more inviting?

FIVE

. . . those obstinate questionings

ST STANISLAUS' COLLEGE, some six miles or so west of
Tullamore, is situated near Rahan, where there are the remains
of a monastery said to have been founded by Camelacus, a
bishop consecrated by no less than St Patrick himself. Here
there is little to be found apart from a very fine Romanesque
window, arch and doorway. The countryside around is flat
with a good deal of bog, some charming rivers, including the
Silver and Little Brosna, and the arrow of the Grand Canal on
its way from Tullamore to the Shannon. Nearby are other
ancient monasteries, notably Clonmacnoise and, within my
own native parish, Clonfert, the See of Saint Brendan.

The college had as nucleus an old house of modest pre-
tensions, to which had been added the usual array of direly
functional school buildings. The ha-ha in front of the original
house reminded one of its earlier aspirations, as did the double
row of trees planted along the demesne wall. There was a small
public chapel beside the college, whose sympathetic confessors
drew penitents from miles around.

The college had a decidedly rural charm. In places there were
old-fashioned and clumsy latches where doorknobs would be
expected. The corridors of bare slabs or boards were immensely
wide, for St Stanislaus' had been a boys' boarding-school in the
nineteenth century and had to handle throngs of boys on rainy
days. But more than that, the sky outside called one out to the

expanse of the countryside. Blessed were they who ventured
forth to watch wild duck and geese and snipe. A few felt blessed
to go in pursuit and shoot them. The plaintive cries of a
stricken lapwing once put an end to such felicity for me.

Coming from pre-war Dublin to wartime Tullabeg gave me
an even greater impression of stepping back into the nineteenth
century. The relatively few cars, buses, and lorries on the
surrounding minor dusty roads got scarcer and scarcer as petrol
was rationed and tyres grew thin. The trains were infrequent
and, because of a shortage of coal, slow and unreliable. One was
cut off in a very real way and depended much on what home
and farm plentifully produced, apart from ersatz coffee. The
sense of battening down against a long war was enhanced by the
return to base of some of our fellows who had gone to study
philosophy in Jersey, to the French province of the Society,
which had a house of studies there. They felt cheated of an
exciting experience.

The impression of retreating to the past was further
reinforced when I looked at the textbooks supplied to us for
some of our courses of study. That for Cosmology, as for some
other subjects, was by Reimer and had been composed in the
first half of the nineteenth century. It was written in Latin, the
language in which were held all our lectures and examinations.
The textbooks for the five other major subjects – Logic
(including Epistemology), Psychology, Ontology, Theodicy
and Ethics – were also in Latin. This brought one back in spirit,
and always in doctrine, to the time of Aquinas. The professor
of Cosmology, a young man brought prematurely back from
specialized studies on the Continent on the outbreak of the war,
struggled conscientiously and with good humour throughout
the year to make our use of Reimer, the scientific basis of which
was centuries out of date – as supplemented by a more recent
textbook, also in Latin, by Hoenan – more or less relevant. But
at the end of the year he felt it necessary to tell us sheepishly

that we had been building bricks with nearly useless straw. It was not for us the altogether disillusioning experience it might have been: he and we knew from the beginning that our tools were not up to the job.

The Logic taught to us was the traditional, and was innocent of anything that might be symbolic. Epistemology was likewise unaffected by all that was happening around us, whether in Vienna or elsewhere. Ontology was taught in a perfunctory and formularly way, by which profound problems were often manipulated at a distance. It was otherwise with Theodicy, where we had a teacher of unusual appearance, character and approach to philosophical problems. He was tall and thin with a long pale face under smoothed black hair. His nose, which he loved to refer to in examples, was his most prominent feature, apart from a pair of bright and mischievous-looking eyes. His attitude to problems was challenging. He assured us that he had tested deeply Aquinas' five proofs for the existence of God and found all of them wanting. There was no hope for any of them, except, perhaps (but not as presented by Aquinas), the fourth, the argument from the possibles. Here he felt that he himself could propose a version of this argument which might just, but only just, save the day. It would be a close-run thing and philosophical atheism threatened him and us at every step. He would then fill the blackboard with his small squiggly script and keep removing or adding items as his exposition of the argument progressed. All the resources of scholasticism, of the commentaries of Cajetan and John of St Thomas and God knows who else, all the subtlest refinements of these authors were drawn upon in the exposition of his views. During the last quarter of an hour the class had a right to ask questions or make comments. In 'Arthur's' class the use of this right was encouraged and fully exercised by a few of my companions who were as mischievous as they were clever. As Arthur had already shown a disposition to question his own philosophic convictions, so he tended to entertain doubts sown by others. Frequently he would withdraw the exposition of some problem, such as that of 'action-at-a-distance', until the morrow, when the whole process might well be repeated. As an exercise in intellectual stimulation, dealing with profound and subtle concepts such as are inherent in scholasticism, for those that were not content merely to juggle with the apparently clear but frequently obscurely rich formulae of Latin terminology and exposition, this was marvellous. But as the professor explained – leaning back in his chair, tightly weaving his long legs over one another, supporting his receding chin on his long pale hands delicately joined together as if in prayer – only a few could profit from his arguments: the rest might compose themselves quietly as best they could. As he said this his eyes laughed secretly and his upper lip smirked happily from one side of his mouth to the other, like a wave curling over upon a slanting shore.

Arthur Little, for that was his name, was sensitive to current thinking in Theodicy and belonged to the succession of internationally known Thomists from Lipperheide and Huit at the turn of the century to Santeler, Fabre, Isaye, Geiger and others up to the Second World War, who began to reveal a great deal more of Plato in Aquinas than had been traditionally ascribed. One of that succession, Durantel, saw in Aquinas an embarrassed Platonist who owed the *best* of his thought to the Pseudo-Dionysius! A continuator, Kremer, in the early seventies had to protest that he was not aiming to reduce the thought of St Thomas to that of Plotinus.

One of the exercises of my course was the writing of a short thesis, as part of the requirements for the award of a doctorate in philosophy from the Gregorian University in Rome. I chose a theme which required me to read the *Enneads* of Plotinus. I naturally chose Arthur as my supervisor. He was deeply sympathetic, encouraging and helpful.

Little did not confine his interests to Theodicy. The qualities which led him to give a number of lectures accounting for the 'origin' of philosophy in Greece as reaction to the bright light and bare rocky character of the country, or (following Valensin, but naturally adding his own peculiar gloss) basing metaphysics on a special concept of the notion of limit, were evident on the tennis court and in the modest orchestra. He was a demon player in both. While I did much more singing in Tullabeg than ever before, I was also the uncomfortable conductor of the orchestra where Arthur was a first violinist. His own pursuit of the correct tempi compelled him to go his own way in spite of the most strenuous efforts to bridle him.

For Psychology we had another serious young man, also returned to us prematurely by the war, who struggled valiantly with ever-reddening face to bring his subject up to date, only to leave himself and us in not a little confusion. It was a disheartening experience, especially for him. The professor of Ethics, also new to the job, fared little better. Here the course was divided into General Ethics and Special Ethics, in which what was taught in the second part was determined by what had been established in the first. Unfortunately the professor, a very decent man, changed his views on General Ethics after some considerable time. It was interesting to note, however, that whereas at the turn of the century to embrace Socialism had been judged a mortal sin, by 1941 it escaped such sanction.

We were given a survey course of the history of Western philosophy by Little in which he preserved a fair balance between the claims of many periods, schools and nations. Eriugena got some, indeed (to judge by many manuals) unusually lengthy, treatment. Descartes got prominence, as did the English empiricists. Berkeley received, naturally, sympathetic interpretation, with more than a passing reference to his ideas on the beneficence of tar-water. The sequence of German philosophers – Leibnitz, Kant, Fichte, Hegel, Schopenhauer,

Nietzsche – was given marked attention.

I had a special interest in (though not love for) Nietzsche. Wilamowitz-Moellendorff, the great classical scholar constantly on Tierney's lips in my university course, had for two years been a contemporary of his at the same boarding-school, Schulpforte, where Wilamowitz on one occasion was tied to a pillar and beaten before the school for the offence of smoking. Nietzsche would have assisted at the humiliating spectacle, which may go some way to explain the venom of Wilamowitz' lifelong hatred of him. For all that, they both fell under the spell of Plato's *Symposium* which they read at Schulpforte. On his seventieth birthday Wilamowitz wrote of his allegiance to Plato:

The kingdom of eternal forms which Plato has opened is indestructible: and we serve it with our scholarship. Into its pure ether the spectres of putrefaction do not penetrate. Hate and Envy are said too to remain outside its divine pale. Under the sign of Plato I shall struggle so long as I have breath. What the boy promised on leaving his beloved mother, Pforte, he will hold to.

Apart from my association of him with Wilamowitz, Nietzsche was associated also with the contemporary and ominous 'philosophy' of the Nazis.

I cannot remember that Little pursued the moderns very far. I remember a little of Husserl and rather more of Bergson who at his death in 1941 is reported to have refrained from converting to Catholicism only to show solidarity with persecuted Jews. There were aspects of his philosophy, especially in relation to metaphysics, which I found very like Heraclitus, and which for me lie near the truth, as I see it: reality is a continuum, not a series of discretes. Language cannot describe reality. There was no whisper that I recollect of Tarski or Carnap. Nor was anything said of Wittgenstein, who visited Ireland at least three times in the thirties, and who was to write, from spring 1948 on, a large part of his *Philosophical Investigations* in Ross's (now the Ashling) hotel in

Parkgate Street, Dublin and in Connemara.

Little did not stress the philosophical approach of the Jesuit Suarez, but did stress minor Jesuit contemporary writers such as Rousselot as against the then fashionable Maritain and the less than tolerant Dominicans: they had wished the Vatican in the early part of this century to *impose* twenty-four important theses in philosophy on Catholic philosophers, but had not succeeded. Scholastics, such as we were, were supposed to be studying philosophy partly at least as a background to the theology that we should encounter later on. But it was taken very seriously in fact in itself, and Jesuits who would be chosen as 'professed fathers' (the élite governing cadre of the Society) were examined on their course in philosophy at the end of their course in theology. It is only when we touched upon questions such as the freedom of the will, however, to which positions on grace were related in theology, that one became conscious that the one was studied as background to the other. In the main the approach was liberal, even if the library (presumably in part for financial reasons) was not extensive or sufficiently representative.

I am happy to say that I enjoyed the course and was grateful for such a comprehensive introduction to philosophical problems, so useful for anyone interested, however modestly, in the life of reason. From what I have described it can be gathered that my reason, though stimulated, was not satisfied. I enjoyed the work, which was shared with many friends. But instead of having less difficulties in relation to faith, I had more, and the passage of time and the continuing challenge of the religious life made them more urgent.

I got some relief from one of the minor courses, which were conducted in the interpretation of texts and anthropology. The professor in the latter subject, who had given us a rather wooden course in ontology, had been in Hong Kong for a number of years, and had there got into public dispute on

religious matters with a local savant. In his efforts to deal with
his opponent he had recourse to his fellow Jesuit Teilhard de
Chardin, then in China, who was known to have extensive
notes prepared on Genesis, the publication of which his Order
discouraged until his death. Teilhard de Chardin had at the
time traversed the Gobi desert in pursuit of evidence for his
palaeontological views, aided by the resources of a remarkable
man called John Galvin whose commercial interests were global
and who later lived in Dublin. Our professor had provided
himself with his colleague's interpretation of *Genesis*, which
dispensed one from understanding it literally: there was room
for some of Darwin. When I shortly afterwards came to read
Augustine's *Genesis Literally Understood*, his third and last effort
to make sense of the Bible story of man's making, written
towards the end of his life, I discovered that in his attempt to
arrive at a *rational* understanding of this fundamental text, he
distinguished between *two* accounts of man's creation in the
first three chapters of Genesis: the one now known as the
Priestly ends (for Augustine) after the fifth verse of the second
chapter, and the other, the Yahwist, continues from there on.
The first account for Augustine, closely following in this the
Neoplatonist Plotinus, describes the making of the *ratio* of man
and woman, the real man and woman. The second, which
contains the story of the making of man from dust and woman
from Adam's rib, speaks of the second 'aspect' of man's making.
On this Augustine comments: 'To think that God modelled
man's body from dust is simply too puerile.' 'Scripture', he
says, 'is using a metaphor.' My encounter with Teilhard de
Chardin was, then, a bit like that of Augustine with Ambrose,
from whom he learned that the spirit gives life, but the letter
death. Many years later, when I was visiting Vassar College, I
dutifully paid a visit in the company of a Jesuit Augustinian
scholar to Teilhard de Chardin's grave in the Jesuit cemetery
at Poughkeepsie beside the Hudson. The Jesuit college there

has now become a catering school. I cannot say that I have ever considered Teilhard de Chardin's 'system' as being persuasive philosophically or theologically. It does, however, develop the notion of the development of the material towards the immaterial, which does appeal to me. And he does not pretend to account for everything. Just as the last sentence of Wittgenstein's *Tractatus* is 'What we cannot speak about we must pass over in silence,' so one of the last sentences of Teilhard de Chardin's *Le phénomène humain* is 'Ce n'est du reste pas le lieu ici, de prendre position.' Teilhard de Chardin's 'system' approaches truth through a kind of poetry.

In spite of whatever relief for my difficulties I found in Teilhard de Chardin, I felt my faith more and more under stress. Also I was especially exercised by the thought that if I were to continue and eventually, after some seven years or so, become an ordained Jesuit I would have to preach the faith to others. This I felt sure, even then, I could not conscientiously do. For the first time, therefore, I asked to see the Provincial with an urgency generated by a feeling of desperation. He kindly invited me to come to see him in Dublin where he assured me, what I already knew, that few escaped this trial of faith, this normal 'night of the soul'. On the basis that he was my superior, who was in the place of God for me, I accepted his assurance, and with him tried to overrule the representations of my own mind. I went back to Tullabeg with a strengthened will but no increased feeling of confidence. I was relieved, however, to know that I did not have to abandon a way of life which I genuinely loved: that of study, good companionship and a common noble purpose.

My pleasant old-fashioned rural existence was thus resumed. I gazed out from the house on the smooth fat cattle, browsing peacefully beyond the ha-ha, up to their dewlaps in the rich buttercup-filled grass. I joined my companions diving and swimming in the Silver, tasting the dark minty water in my mouth. Swimming in a river has a special and most pleasurable sensation. We rowed our heavy craft along the canal, feeling the fresh and fragrant winds from over the bogs upon our faces. When we made for the relatively distant Little Brosna or Shannon, we shortened the time spent at the many locks by portaging our cumbrous and leaden boats, an unreasonable tax upon our physical resources. The reward, however, when we got to the great river or crossed to the canal and Clonfert on the western side, and saw the white water-lilies there and the wonderful doorway of the Cathedral, was worth the very real pains. Some, I think, got up the river as far as Clonmacnoise, 'Saint Kieran's city fair'.

I cannot pass on without saying a little more of the bogland in this area. My experience of it in 1939-41 is well exemplified in David Bellamy's celebration *The Wild Boglands* (1986):

It was January 1959, and the frost jewelled both the callow and the bogs up to Tullamore. The surface of each bog was frozen still and it seemed sacrilege to break such perfection. We waited till the warmth of a duck-egg blue day had melted the rime. Then across the steaming bog we saw a sight of immense beauty and rarity. Skein upon skein of Greenland white-fronted geese rose from the bog where they had spent the night in safety and made their way down to the callow to graze.

Many of us were already enthralled by R. L. Praeger's *The Way That I Went* (1937), an essential book for one who would know the beauty of Ireland. We traversed the bogs, jumping from hummock to hummock, identifying everything we saw. Some may know of the beauty of bogland in late summer, when there is a rich carpet of purple for miles around, but few seem to realize its appeal in the winter when in the early morning it wears the magical rime under an open sky of which Bellamy speaks.

In the new year of 1940 we had a long period of frost during which our professors, very humanely, either cancelled classes altogether for the day, or arranged them suitably, so that we might skate from morning until dark on a lake on the Charleville demesne some four or five miles distant. The simple joys of country living! It was divine. Our collection of skates, scarce in number, haphazard in fitting on to our walking-boots, and rusty from being mostly unused over many years, provided us with unspoiled delight. The trudge home over the narrow unmetalled roads under a radiant moon gave one the feeling that one had escaped from time.

In June 1940 we had our 'major villa' (main holiday) in Roundstone on the west coast of Galway. This time we had no spacious accommodation, but were crowded into a rather small house under Errisbeg. We swam in the sparkling sea and bicycled all over the glorious countryside, and generally led a wholly extrovert existence. One excursion I well recall. It entailed a bicycle ride of about thirty-five miles to Killary, crossing Killary Harbour in a curragh and then climbing up Mweelrea (2688') in swirling clouds, a dangerous and (counting the return journey) tiring exploit, but very satisfying. When we were not admiring the spectacular scenery with its rare colourings and unique quality of light, we kept looking out to sea, half expecting a German landing which had been rumoured. Our seaside idyll, however, was without interruption.

During my second year in Tullabeg we had a new Rector, Donal O'Sullivan, an enthusiast, who had been captivated by Austria, where he had done four years of theology, and commended constantly the sacred art of Maria Laach and the doctrine of the mystical body. I found his enthusiasm slightly overpowering which led, naturally, to some reaction within me. But he was a good man who began, then, to promote the rehabilitation of prisoners. His approach to art, too, became more sophisticated. In due course he acquired for Tullabeg five Evie Hone stained-glass windows of which three at least are very fine. Later he was to become chairman of the Arts Council and did a great deal to promote painting in Ireland.

The doctrine of the mystical body, the doctrine that Christ lives in us, requires great faith to practise over any length of time. It demands a sense of actuality which pushes faith to the extreme. Our Rector, as he walked around in a long black buckled cloak (very infrequently sported by Jesuits of the Irish Province) and biretta, seemed constantly engaged in happy communion. I on the other hand wanted not to challenge faith, to let it quietly lie. His good example was for me discouraging.

At the end of the year the Provincial sent me (and ten others) to teach at Clongowes Wood College, a boarding-school in County Kildare. It was thought that Jesuits at this stage in their lengthy preparation, involving so much prolonged study, would benefit from engaging not in learning, but in teaching; in giving rather than receiving; in practical life, not theoretical. I felt that the disaffection with faith that I lived with might, perhaps, be eased in a life in which I had the distraction of working for others. I looked forward to the change with anticipation of relief and so not a little joy.

★ ★ ★

Clongowes Wood College, Clongowes for short, was one of the first, if not the first, of the colleges opened by the Jesuits in 1814 shortly after their restoration. In the intervening period it has become known as the Alma Mater of a very respectable 'Rogues' Gallery' of politicians, revolutionaries, diplomats, bishops, professors and literary artists, the best known of the last being James Joyce. In the Ireland of the nineteenth and early twentieth centuries, it provided education to the growing number of increasingly comfortable and ambitious Catholics, who otherwise would have felt it necessary to go to Stoneyhurst or Downside, in England, for a public-school education. It has produced and continues to produce a significant quota of the professional classes in the State.

The school is situated in extensive wood-fringed grounds

with a near and smiling prospect of the Dublin mountains some fifteen miles over the circling Liffey to the east. The nucleus of the college was an old border fort of the English Pale, which had been altered in the eighteenth century and was known as Castle Browne when the Jesuits purchased it. Additions were made over the years, especially in the early 1930s when an immense line of expensive battlemented buildings in cut stone gave the college a very impressive appearance indeed. The boys' chapel contains interesting Stations of the Cross by Sean Keating and some fine stained-glass windows by Michael Healy and Evie Hone.

The school was divided into three 'Lines' or sections, the Upper embracing the bigger boys in their last two years or so, the 'Lower' an intermediate group, and the 'Third' boys up to about fourteen years of age. Each line had its own playing-fields and sports pavilion, library, dormitories and Jesuit prefect – a priest each for the two upper lines. There was strict segregation of the lines and the Third had its own study. My contact with the boys as a master was almost entirely confined to the class-room, although I did take each of the lines separately to the swimming-pool before breakfast, and refereed less ambitious rugby matches in the Lower Line. Not only, then, was there segregation among the boys, but they were in practice to some extent separated from most of the Jesuits, priests or scholastics, also. This may have had some advantages, but it deprived the boys of the general educational and cultural influence of a large body of highly trained men. It was part of the Jesuit system of discipline, which proscribed 'particular friendships'.

The course of studies had to take account of the organization of public education in Ireland and the Matriculation require-ments of the universities, particularly those of the National University of Ireland. There remained something, nevertheless, of the old *Ratio Studiorum* which had made the Jesuits at one time the most famous educators throughout Europe. This was to be seen, for example, in the names given to the class-years or forms. The sixth form was called 'Rhetoric', the fifth 'Poetry', and so on down through 'Syntax' and 'Grammar' to 'Rudiments' and 'Elements'. The scholastics also got a course in education, in Latin, from Timothy Corcoran, the Jesuit professor of Education in University College, Dublin, in which the ideals and practices of Jesuit education, embodied in the *Ratio Studiorum*, were strongly emphasized.

I want to say *en passant* that the observation of this particular Jesuit professor of education was of much interest to me. He had been a successful teacher as a scholastic in Clongowes and had, it was rumoured, applied for the chair of education in University College, Dublin without the knowledge of his superiors who, when he won it, would have found it difficult, not to say injudicious, to do anything about such an attractive *fait accompli*. He was not, however, elevated at the time to the grade of professed father, as might have been expected. A pronounced nationalist, he had edited the *Catholic Bulletin*, a republican journal, about the time of the Rebellion in 1916. As professor of education he attracted an immense number of teachers from all over the country who supported him ardently in university elections, as he did them in their professional advancement. It was he who assured the new State that the Irish language, of which, I believe, he knew little, could be revived in five years. There was a story abroad in University College that one required influence to fail his particular examinations. Certainly the results were returned to the Supervisor rather speedily. Elaborate examination papers were set, made up wholly of passages in Greek, for Greekless post-graduate students, who, however, knew what to write about from the few words in English given as a legend at the top of the passage. These examination papers were sent to continental institutions and Rome for their wondering admiration. In the end he is said to have been elevated to the professed grade of the Society by Rome.

I knew him mostly from the course in education which he gave in Clongowes, but also because I was asked, as he was then an elderly man, to shave him every morning while he was in Clongowes. During the course he became almost apoplectic when one scholastic gently drew to his attention that his percentages did not add up to a hundred. Our examination was something of a show-piece too. Although we had six papers of six questions each and in Latin, our answers, also in Latin, to all the questions seemed unavoidably to be much the same. But we did not fail, nor for that matter gain distinction! When I went to shave him each morning I waited outside his door (I suspect not without his knowledge) until a nearby clock was about to sound the last stroke of nine, with which my first knock then exactly coincided. When I was bidden in, I always found him installed in a chair, ready for the operation. As I came in, he struck his thigh loudly with his open hand and asked with an empurpled laugh, 'What bit of gossip can I regale you with to-day?' He loved precision, though he wrote abominably, and had plenty of humour.

To return to the school: all its staff were well qualified, and studies and games were highly organized, but there was no effort to compete closely with other schools in either the one or the other. Being a school with a relatively long tradition, the practices and attitudes of nineteenth-century British schools had not wholly disappeared. A few of the older priests remained rather British in outlook. Cricket was played throughout the school. A boy might still, however rarely, be beaten on his exposed buttocks by the Rector with a heavy strap. A serious effort was made to inculcate religion, but there was no question of indulging in excessive zeal. The excesses in which I had been involved in Garbally were unimaginable here. Clongowes was not a seminary: it prepared for the world.

I enjoyed Clongowes even if, because it was my first

experience of it, I found teaching rather tiring. I was given a fair sample of mostly Greek and Latin classes throughout the school, but naturally found the most senior and most junior boys (so bright and eager) the most rewarding. But, as I said, outside the class-room I had little contact with the students.

On the other hand I had for the first time unrestricted daily contact, not only with my fellow scholastics, but with all the priests in the community, that is in the ninth year since I joined the Jesuits. They were fine men for much the greater part and good companions. They had their idiosyncrasies and played on one another with for the most part great good humour. A few seemed under strain. A few others seemed not to have a care in the world.

Among these latter was Cyril Power, the man in charge of the large farm, who had a deep laugh and a broad jovial face. He had won a travelling studentship in mathematics to Downing College in Cambridge in earlier years, and had subsequently been professor of theology and Rector of a theologate. It was said (but it never seemed possible to confirm such things) that he had declined to become Provincial of the Order in Ireland and so had either been sent, or had asked to go, to Clongowes as farmer and to do a little teaching of mathematics on the side. His responsibilities required him to go to Dublin about once a week, when he shed his chalky gown and mucky wellington boots. If I were free, as happened from time to time, he invited me, sometimes with another scholastic, to meet him for lunch at a modest hotel in Dublin and then accompany him to the cinema. I cannot remember that I had been to the cinema – nor for that matter had ordinary access to a radio or gramophone – for nine years nor, I think, had I been in a restaurant in the same period. These trips to Dublin with the farmer could not have been more innocent, but they had a new touch of worldliness for me. It was a further late debriefing from the intensities of the novitiate.

One of the priests, the senior master in Classics, was rather a rough diamond, but diamond he was. As I taught Classics I was necessarily thrown a lot together with him, especially as we both loved to walk out through the countryside. He never went through a gate if he could jump or hoist himself over it, so robust and vigorous was he of body. Likewise he was robust and vigorous in his mind and its expression. He had studied for several years in Spain during the civil war there and was a fanatical admirer of Franco. In Clongowes where the community as a whole was anti-Nazi in the Second World War, and a few frankly British, he thundered out his admiration for the Axis powers on every possible occasion. He inflicted these views on me on our walks, to the point that I felt limp and exhausted when we got home. I consulted the Spiritual Father on what I should do. I did not at all sympathize with this Jesuit's views, but I felt it did him good to let off steam, even at my expense. The Spiritual Father saw nothing wrong with this. But I soon discovered that I could be branded with guilt by association. When I appeared before the Rector at the regular interval to 'manifest my conscience', he asked me, just when we were finished, if I was not consorting over-much with Father so-and-so who gave expression to very vehement views. I reported to him my attitude and that I had raised the matter with the Spiritual Father. He appeared to take the same view and shrugged the whole thing off with an indulgent smile. It was clear that some other Jesuit had felt obliged to 'manifest' my fault. I found the situation disagreeable from every point of view, but did no more than limit my exposure as best I could. But Stalingrad had not yet fallen when I left Clongowes.

The only serious reading I did during my year in Clongowes was a number of the volumes of Leopold von Ranke's *History of the Popes*, and H. Brémond's *Histoire littéraire du sentiment religieux en France*. To be truthful, the libraries, both for all the Lines and for the staff, had suffered some inanition since Ireland had separated itself from the richer United Kingdom and had no longer to compete with some of its schools. I do not now remember if I got these books on loan, but in any case I read them. I suppose that on the whole I found the history of the Popes, even as so presented, not highly inciting to the life of faith, and Brémond's marvellous volumes tended for me to increase the appeal of literature somewhat at the expense of spirituality. But I suffered no great crisis. Although I felt that I was drifting further away from my spiritual convictions, I was unwilling to challenge my Superior's view that all was normal – as indeed it must have seemed to my companions. Augustine in his *Confessions*, speaking of his own numbness of will, dwells on those 'who want to arouse themselves but, still overcome by deep drowsiness, sink back again. Just as no man would want to sleep forever, and it is the sane judgment of all men that it is better to be awake, yet a man often defers to shake off sleep when a heavy languor pervades all his members, and although the time to get up has come, he yields to it with pleasure even although it now irks him.' Moreover I was to have a new experience. I was going to Oxford on the travelling studentship I had won. Who knows how it might affect me? I felt myself that it would, so to speak, make or break me. I had observed the drift within my own mind and it did not bode well. Yet strange things happen. I was sorry to leave Clongowes where there was so much to please me. I was able even to exercise a pony from time to time and loved my draughty room in the tower off the community library. I departed for Oxford with a little hope but much greater anticipation.

SIX

What though the radiance which was
once so bright
Be now for ever taken from my sight, . . .
We will grieve not, rather find
Strength in what remains behind.

I GREATLY REGRET having to say it, but the sensation of freedom I felt on landing from the boat on the unlovely railway platform of Holyhead early in October 1942, when the critical, and perceived even then to be critical, battle of Stalingrad was still undecided, filled me with a new happiness. The heavy smell of coal in the air, being addressed as 'Love' by the barmaid in the restaurant as she slopped over a cup of cold tannin-filled tea to me, and all the evidences of a country at total war could not dim my joy in feeling simply anonymous in a more open society. The oppression of an introverted, neutral, and simplistic Ireland where lost causes, such as the revival of the Irish language, were explicitly and relentlessly pursued had weighed upon my spirit. In such a religious hothouse one had difficulty in maintaining a human choice. But I felt an almost physical oppression too. On a number of occasions I had counted the clerics I met going the length of one side of O'Connell Street in Dublin. It averaged a dozen, to say nothing about the nuns, and we were constantly being saluted. I had become allergic to clerics in those conditions.

I was met at the railway station in Oxford, in the black-out, late at night. We trundled my bags through the black wet streets, sensing the smell of coal from the gasworks. It was not enlivening. Yet I felt happy and reassured to be in the city so favourably and beautifully described by Gerard Manley

Hopkins. Matthew Arnold's tribute: 'Beautiful city! so vener-
able, so lovely . . . spreading her gardens to the moonlight', was
still for me powerful in its evocation. Only too relevant for me
seemed likely to be his 'home of lost causes and forsaken beliefs
. . . and impossible loyalties'.

Soon we found ourselves in Brewer Street, making our way
along by the southern wall of Pembroke College, and then let
ourselves in to Campion Hall. This is a Permanent Private Hall
intended mainly for Jesuits who are members of the University,
who, as its residents, enjoy similar rights in the University to
those enjoyed by members of Colleges.

Campion Hall incorporated Micklem Hall, an old private
Hall once used by a prominent old Catholic family. Sir Edwin
Lutyens designed the new hall alongside the old, both in close
proximity to the Catholic Chaplaincy in the Old Palace in Rose
Place. It was situated, therefore, beside the Choir School of
Christ Church and so beside the House itself. Lutyens was a
constant visitor in my time, an old man sucking a very small
pipe, needing to be entertained, that is, to have a patient
audience for an endless series of *risqué* stories. He spoke to me
a little from time to time about his mother, who had been at
a convent school in Kerry, and of at least five commissions in
Ireland, especially Lambay Castle, which incorporated an older
castle where Archbishop Ussher wrote several of his works.
Ussher it was who had tautologously and confusingly labelled
the philosopher-theologian, on whom I had proposed eventually
to work, Scottus Eriugena ('Irish of Irish birth'), now referred
to simply and more correctly as Eriugena. I saw the castle many
years later when Lord Revelstoke allowed me to bring a party
there to visit the site of Roman burials on the island. In the
meantime I was to enjoy Lutyens's many pranks in Campion
Hall, including the rose in the ceiling of the dining hall, where
Jesuits, as the Eyres in Eyrecourt, conversed *sub rosa*. Less
amusing was the aircraft light components factory which, in

this constricted site, ran parallel to Campion Hall and from which emanated popular music, notably 'Workers' Playtime' every morning at 9 a.m. How fortunate we were that the deafening and monotonous cacophony, the apparently painful freneticism of our later times had not arrived! 'We'll Gather Lilacs' or even 'Roll out the Barrel' at least had a tune.

Campion Hall on the inside was full, it was said, of *objets d'Arcy*, this in reference to the well-known aesthetic and collecting proclivities of its charming Master, Martin C. D'Arcy, sj. There were some good pieces and pictures elsewhere throughout the house, but the *pièce de résistance* was the chapel itself. Here Lutyens had contrived both an imposing wooden screen and *baldacchino* in quite a small space, which I found very pleasing. Off the chancel was a small side-chapel of Our Lady, the walls of which, during all the time I was there, were being decorated, so as to depict not only the Virgin but members of the Hall, by a red-headed painter with an Irish name. He spoke little and was thought not to be overpoweringly given to theology. He appeared to make slow progress, for he constantly changed his drawings. The sacristy contained among other items interesting chasubles, a few Elizabethan, and at least one made from a Japanese kimono adorned with fertility motifs. The Sacristan consulted with the Master each evening as to which he would wear at Mass on the morrow. The Master wore all of them more or less in sequence. I admired his 'balance' between the preservation and use of antiques.

The Master was one of the most intelligent, liberal and warm-hearted men that it has been my lot to know. His earlier interests are indicated by the title of a book of his, *The Nature of Belief*. By the time I knew him his interest had shifted somewhat towards aestheticism and mysticism, *erōs* and *agapē*, on which topics especially he loved to draw out his guests in the Senior Common Room. This was in the old Micklem Hall. Its dark oak panelling provided a sharp background to the bright vermilion chairs prescribed by Lutyens. Here, almost nightly, the Master entertained many of the interesting people that visited Oxford. The port, appropriately, was neither very old nor very copious, but the conversation was, usually, good and elevating. On one side of the fireplace sat D'Arcy with his wavy grey locks, piercing black eyes under beetling eyebrows, mobile, rather cavernous face and light black Jesuit gown over the neatest pair of shoes. There was a portrait of him by Augustus John in the dining hall which I thought very good. And on my first visit to the Museum of Modern Art in New York I found him fixing me with his eye from one of its walls. He was eminently paintable. Picasso might in earlier days have 'invented' him.

On the other side of the fireplace was often to be found the almost mute (on these occasions) persona of Ronnie Knox. There was, of course, a constant stream of the more prominent Catholics; among others Frederick Copleston, Christopher Dawson, Douglas Woodruff, Alfred Noyes, and Evelyn Waugh. The last, accompanied by batman, sometimes stayed in the Hall. He was much frustrated by disappointment with his limited military role, which did not live up to the splendour of his dress uniform. He looked arrogant and spoke arrogantly. Another visitor who lingers much in my memory was an old and enfeebled Hilaire Belloc. He had by this time got beyond speaking much, which allowed him to concentrate with what energy remained to him upon the wine: he lived up to his 'philosophy' to the end. Frank Pakenham (now the Earl of Longford), then a 'Student' at Christ Church and involved in selling the Beveridge Plan, which introduced much of the Socialism of modern Britain, was constantly in and out, consulting Lewis ('Lucy') Watt on points of Catholic Social Theory. Frank always succeeded in looking *distrait*, and I think he always was. Among occasional visitors were Roy Campbell, Stephen Spender, Neville Coghill, Shane Leslie, John Rothenstein (whose American wife, Elizabeth, was doing murals in the basement), a famous collector of jade, and a descendant of an Irish 'Wild Geese' family loyal to the Stuarts (a toast to these was drunk with discreet solemnity every year). Many of the stream of lecturers who visited Oxford found their way to Campion Hall, attracted by D'Arcy's local reputation and the greater intimacy of a small institution, where the war-time food might receive on occasion that little more attention.

D'Arcy's method in discussion was to introduce some topic, on which he was currently writing a book, and have it thrashed out for several hours. He spoke much himself, so that the points he was concerned with got full attention. As I was studying both Augustine and Neoplatonism at the time and these were relevant to subsequent mysticism at least, if not also in a lesser way to aestheticism, he liked to have me present as a respondent of last resort. When the party had broken up, the Master would repair to his room and address himself to his writing. In this way was gestated and written *The Mind and Heart of Love*, a sequel to Nygren's *Erōs and Agapē*. D'Arcy's books were no longer 'scholarly': his energy was too low for that; but neither were they 'popular'. Some years later the wife of a colleague of mine told me that her maid, looking for something light and romantic to read on her night in, picked up *The Mind and Heart of Love*, which to her somewhat shocked surprise she found in my friend's study, and went happily to her kitchen, thinking that she had just the thing. I could not but smile wryly, remembering D'Arcy's rather esoteric discussions. His conversation was better than his books.

The Senior Tutor was Leslie Walker, a burly, grumpy-looking but actually good-humoured man with shaggy yellow-white hair and a deeply creased face. This lit up with a warm and radiant smile, whenever, as happened often, he was in hot pursuit of something that puzzled him in the Greek text of Aristotle's *Metaphysics*. He was not the only eccentric in

Campion Hall. There were about a dozen scholastics other than myself there, who were members of the University. We all had our tuition in the Colleges, and some students from the Colleges came for tuition to Campion Hall. Students of Westfield College, London, had been evacuated to Oxford during the war and I myself was asked to give tutorials in Greek philosophy to some of these. Tutors were not plentiful in war-time Oxford.

When I had been duly matriculated I was sent by the Senior Tutor to see Raymond Klibansky to arrange that he supervise me for the D. Phil. degree. Klibansky was then a young man with a great reputation. I was happy to find him sympathetic and helpful, and all appeared to be satisfactorily arranged for my study of Neoplatonism in Augustine. But he proved to be elusive, for he suddenly joined Intelligence in London, and that was the end of his supervising.

I was then passed on to Richard Walzer, whose intellectual lineage went back through Werner Jaeger to Wilamowitz-Moellendorff. He was one of a notable group of Classical Philologists who were refugees in Oxford, and had been attached to Oriel, where the Vice-Chancellor, Sir David Ross, was Provost. Ross was a foremost Aristotelian scholar and knew Walzer from the latter's *Magna Moralia und Aristotelische Ethik* and *Dialogues* (of Aristotle). He invited Walzer to Oriel. Having been disappointed about Klibansky, I was sent to Ross to have his advice on a new tutor. While I was waiting upon the Vice-Chancellor, inside the door of the Provost's Lodge, Lady Ross attempted to profit from my idle hands by proffering me a duster and inviting me to set to! Unfortunately for her housework, or perhaps fortunately for her bric-à-brac, her husband came out to me almost immediately. After some discussion he suggested that I should take the required fortnightly supervision from Walzer, for whom he wished to provide some duties. Neither Ross nor Walzer pretended that the latter was then an expert in either Neoplatonism or Augustine, much less both.

The Regius Professor of Greek, the Irishman Eric Dodds, a first-class Neoplatonist scholar who had done an important article on Augustine's *Confessions* in the *Hibbert Journal* some years before, was not available for various reasons, principally because of a projected lengthy visit to China under the auspices of the Government. But I soon became friendly with Dodds with whose wife I worked on providing a book service to prisoners of war. Although I had been warned against him as a 'dangerous atheist' by an academic Jesuit in Dublin, I found him to be an agnostic with strong religious interests (as appears indeed from his published works, especially his edition of Euripides' *Bacchae*), of a liberal and sympathetic outlook, and with an intelligent and strong continuing interest in Irish affairs (although for long he lived in 'Cromwell's House'!). I invited him to Dublin in later years and was in correspondence with him until his death. He helped me unofficially in many ways in my studies in Oxford and subsequently, and was a non-intrusive and discreet adviser in other problems. His sheer honesty, even *naïveté*, reveals itself in his autobiography, *Missing Persons*, which is, I think, excessively modest. He had not been welcomed to Oxford as Regius Professor of Greek and this left some shadow over his long life there.

Richard Walzer was one of a number of truly noble Jews (Harold Cherniss was another) whom I was blessed to know. He also was an innocent abroad. Although when I first met him, his English was halting and he was versed in neither Plotinus, Porphyry nor Augustine, he was determined to give me all the service he could. Accordingly he supervised me weekly instead of fortnightly, and extended the session from the required one to two hours. He started from what he knew, that is Ocellus Lucanus, a philosopher listed as a Pythagorean by the Neoplatonist Iamblichus. A treatise on the *Nature of the All*, which shows considerable traces of Aristotelian influence and is to be dated probably to the first century BC, is, perhaps wrongly, attributed to Ocellus Lucanus. This treatise had been edited by R. Harder, whose already distinguished work on Plotinus was known, of course, to Walzer. Harder was tainted with Nazism. Walzer moved carefully. He took refuge in meticulousness, which in any case came naturally to him, and his help to me was doubtless fundamental but meagre to my perception.

He suffered the inconvenience of having present at our linguistically painful sessions his robust, ebullient and masterful wife, a member of the well-known Cassirer family. She interrupted as she pleased, asking if I would come to dinner to them with Billy Pantin (also of Oriel), or bring her some chocolates from Ireland to eke out the English ration which she found inadequate, or teach Richard the art of riding a bicycle, or bring them both punting on the Cherwell. On one or two occasions she darned her stockings *in situ* which met with furtive scowling, but no comment, from her disapproving and distracted spouse. I tried to comply in due course with all her wishes, but not in any instance, except the chocolates, to her satisfaction or mine. A few of the generously prepared dinner parties were aborted by air-raid signals, sending Pantin and myself scurrying to do our stints in firewatching. I never succeeded in getting Richard to balance himself on my bicycle, try as I might to lean against or pull away in compensation for his determined lunge to left or right down many an Oxford street. And not surprisingly we never made the social grade on the bewitching Cher. The life of a refugee, despite all the generous efforts by the host community, was not easy, and I had much sympathy at the time for Mrs Walzer, and great admiration for the true scholar that her husband was.

At the end of the year with Walzer I asked to have a new Supervisor, although I was warned that 'it was dangerous to change horses in mid-stream'. I took the risk. Walzer, who was really interested then in Galen, was as relieved as I was. We parted on the best of terms. Later, when I was already a professor, settled in Dublin, he kindly tried to induce me to interest myself in a position in Oxford, where he had now established himself well and become an expert in early Islamic philosophy. It was my last dealing with him.

My new tutor was reported to be 'the most learned man in the university'. He was Claude Jenkins, Canon of Christ Church and Regius Professor of Ecclesiastical History. He features, justly, in books that touch on notable eccentrics of Oxford towards the middle of this century. He lived in rooms in Tom Quad near the cathedral, rooms that immediately assailed one's nostrils with the smell of cats and spilt milk, and one's eyes with an avalanche of books. Dacre Balsdon in *Oxford Now and Then* describes how the House finally decided that his rooms and his garden, beginning more easily with the latter, should be cleaned up. When confronted on this by the Dean, the Canon is reported to have replied with self-satisfaction, 'I have done something already. I have had it declared a bird sanctuary!' While I have many remembrances of Jenkins I mostly see him making his way along St Aldate's to or from Carfax. Usually he appears in his black shovel hat over a rather Pickwickian face, the rest of him clothed bulkily in a heavy black coat topped by a bright loose macintosh. He has bread under his arm and one suspects him of munching it as he goes along.

When I presented myself in his rooms at a time arranged in the *second* week of the eight-week Michaelmas term of 1943, I made my way to the Canon, sitting in an armchair before a fire, along a fairway cleared through the floor of books. This was effected by transferring them on to the bed, whence they would be again transferred when the Canon gave himself formally to sleep. I had no sooner at his bidding occupied a chair islanded beside him than he informed me in plain and matter-of-fact

terms that I represented for him three of the things he hated
most: a Jesuit, a Roman Catholic and an Irishman. As an
Irishman I am well accustomed to the irony of understanding
the opposite of what is said to me and of saying the opposite
of what I mean, but not so as to be misunderstood. I was swiftly
reassured when he said with a quizzical smile: 'Now, we'll get
on well together, I presume!' He got to the point immediately:
had I an essay to read to him? I had drafted some chapters of
my proposed thesis which had the unlovely but carefully
provident title of 'Prolegomena to the *Contra Academicos* of Saint
Augustine'. I proceeded to read a chapter to him, but soon
noticed that he was noisily asleep. I stopped reading until he
should wake. I hesitated to waken him. After a long interval I
quietly withdrew. I next presented myself in the fourth week
of term to be greeted with the disarming avowal: 'Well! we did
not make much progress on the last occasion. Let's try again.'
I started on the same chapter, he promptly fell asleep, and I as
promptly came away. In the sixth week of term he started by
declaring that, as we had made even less progress on the last
occasion, we should take precautions on this. It was, of course,
a shared endeavour. He gave, he said, a series of lectures on
Greek Palaeography on Wednesdays in the Chapter House at 10
a.m., that is, he explained, at 10.15 a.m. Greenwich time, but
10.10 a.m. in Christ Church. I might get some profit from his
tuition if I attended. Eager to profit, I said I would. Would I,
then, read my 'essay' again? I started, he nodded, I left. In the
seventh week of term I waited outside the Chapter House until
the hour appointed when he appeared in the cloister in bulky
academicals (including bands) and a large sheaf of yellowing
notes. I preceded him into the large room and seated myself, the
only one there, just below the rostrum. As he passed forwards
by me he inclined away and bowed towards me with surpassing
grace. Arrived at the rostrum, he rolled up the bookstand to a
height convenient to him, placed his notes heavily upon it and

then, after a silence-inducing pause, exclaimed aloud: 'Gentle-men!' He glanced briefly towards me with a winning smile and then proceeded to read somebody else's notes (as I understood) dealing with Archbishop Laud. I continued to attend this course in 'Greek Palaeography' (for which, I was told, perhaps wrongly, he was paid a special stipend) for the rest of the year, but was quietly allowed to abandon supervision. There were few students engaged in post-graduate studies in Oxford then and indeed the University did not feel that it should greatly concern itself with or make much provision for them. Jenkins and myself, however, had frequent and for me helpful corre-spondence during vacations, some of which at least he spent at Malvern Wells in Worcestershire. He was on occasion at least a stickler for formality, and his appearance, with C. C. J. Webb, in the Chapter House for my viva was as awe-inspiring as bright-plumed academic formality could make it.

Meanwhile my thesis on Neoplatonism and Saint Augustine proceeded slowly, but surely, with Dodds's discreet advice and long sessions in Duke Humphrey's Library (where a friendly librarian expedited books to me, then a truly great service). I also used Pusey House, where F. L. Cross, later Lady Margaret Professor of Divinity at Christ Church and instigator of the enormously successful International Conference on Patristic Studies, still presided over by Miss E. A. Livingstone, was a serious presence ever flitting between the stacks. It was while reading over the tenth book of Augustine's *City of God* in the *Corpus Scriptorum Ecclesiasticorum Latinorum* while leaning against these same stacks one day that a thought occurred to me. It was that Augustine's conversion was, among other influences in a complex and lengthy development, particularly affected by Porphyry's eager search for a mediator between God and man; his consideration of Christ as that mediator; and his rejection of him on account of his birth of a woman and death on the cross. Augustine was persuaded that Porphyry had come very close to becoming a Christian, but had been prevented by demons (who were more real to Augustine and his contemporaries than we can even imagine) and Neoplatonist pride, which could not stomach God becoming man. Part of his own conversion, then, was in reaction to Porphyry's decision. To him it seemed that Neoplatonism, uncorrupted by demonology and tamed of pride, and the Scriptures pointed to Christ as the Mediator through whom man could be saved. Augustine had something of a penchant for discovering unexpected, indeed paradoxical, developments within his own life and the lives of others. Those 'who came to scoff, remained to pray'. Thus was Saint Paul converted, who set out breathing fire to persecute the Christians only to end by suddenly joining them. So Augustine himself came to listen only to the eloquence of Saint Ambrose, but ended by accepting his message. He saw Providence in all things. Grace was everywhere. Hence Augustine speaks as a matter of fact more and more favourably of Porphyry than Plotinus, bewails his fate, and sets out to win over his followers, his own contemporaries. Then all would be one.

At the time of my consideration of this matter, the prevailing fashion among the relatively few scholars of Neoplatonism of the day, who accepted for the most part the exotic and unfavourable opinion of Porphyry given by J. Bidez in his *Vie de Porphyre*, saw almost the whole, if not all, of the Neoplatonist influence exerted upon Augustine at his conversion as coming directly from Plotinus. This was the view of Paul Henry, later to become a friend. Dodds tended in this direction too. But W. Theiler of Berne, later accepted as a great Neoplatonist scholar, had argued strongly that Porphyry was the almost sole influence, and I felt that his arguments, as happens for a point of view different from one received (for many 'established'), had not been examined with sufficient care and objectivity. But I did not minimize the role of Plotinus.

Even as I was quite independently writing my thesis in England, Pierre Courcelle in a France separated by war was revealing in 1943 how the more important Neoplatonist influence on Augustine was Porphyry. But this and other attendant controversies have no further place here. The dispute earned a protracted, heated but delightful discussion at the Congrès International Augustinien in Paris in 1954 under the endearingly excited *présidence* of Paul Henry (*Augustinus Magister* III 27-50). On that occasion our seriousness collapsed when one of the French clerical disputants shouted back at Henry: 'Flûte pour Plotin!' Henry had a big heart and enjoyed the fun.

Apart from the lectures of Jenkins, 'related to my course', I sampled whatever was on offer in the fields of Classics and Medieval Philosophy and Theology. Much more was on offer in the former. My great experience here was being accepted into the seminar on Aeschylus' *Agamemnon* conducted by Eduard Fraenkel. Most of the audience were dons. Fraenkel assigned each of us a portion of the work which we had to explicate on a particular day following. We had plenty of time to prepare. He was merciless in his criticism of every one of us so that I, at least, felt pretty inadequate, although I had done relatively recently an intense basic study of the text, including its *apparatus criticus*, with Tierney in Dublin. Fraenkel stood at the head of the table over us and barked his unnerving observations on our evidently stupid efforts. The harsh experience was made worse by the contemplation of his damaged arm. Was he compensating for that and much else? But, no! It was a method where concessions were *not* made. When one spoke to him away from the seminar he showed himself helpful and understanding, and amazingly erudite. I can remember putting detailed questions to him on the readings of other, Latin, texts without any notice whatever: he was able to quote the lines in question and the relevant readings straight off without reference to any book. His humanity is even emotionally apparent in his book on Horace: there his feeling for the poet and the poet's father overflows the mould of erudition. There is a warmth that one can hardly expect in a book of this kind. He unbends too and treats one to some gay rococo writing. It was no surprise to me that he would not survive his wife.

I attended Cyril Bailey's course on Lucretius, J. D. Beazley on Classical Art, and Maurice Bowra on Greek lyric poetry, which was not sparkling, in contrast to his occasional performances at literary societies. I remember his starting off one such by declaring that the poet X's mother was 'of no uncertain character' which was a mild beginning to what was to follow. I recollect Hugh Last, frequently in spats, seeming solemnly to ignore at the beginning of his lecture a tribute of a few long tulips – perhaps from an admirer on some anniversary – laid forward on his rostrum. Gradually he took notice and raised them towards his face by the middle of the lecture, and then as gradually laid them down towards the end. His lectures were very much worth while. He received me on a number of occasions in Brasenose, whose Principal was W. T. S. Stallybrass, a name appropriate to his College and changed from Sonnenschein. There was a head of Eriugena at the entrance to the Hall of BNC which was in much need of the repairs since done. And I have looked on Gilbert Murray lecturing, and on Lady Mary eagerly looking back upon the audience to encourage its approval. He was still content in Oxford before the changes wrought there by the education act of 1944 and the ending of the war. I attended some 'popular' lectures such as those of G. D. H. Cole: one can hardly realize now how vibrant discussions of economics were in Oxford then. It was remarkable that in the middle of a perilous, indeed catastrophic war, England spent so much of its time debating Beveridge and Butler. I was deeply impressed by this and, for all the debate, of the extraordinary feeling of unity in the population. It was marvellously exhilarating.

There were other ways of imbibing information than through supervision, reading, lectures and calling upon individual scholars for help generously given – such as I got from H. H. Price on logic, in connection with Augustine's *Contra Academicos*, and F. Homes Dudden in relation to Saint Ambrose. There was the plethora of societies where papers were discussed. Of these the one of which I have the liveliest remembrance is the Philological, which was mainly for dons and met in Christ Church. It was dominated by refugees who normally divided into two fiercely opposing sections. F. Jacoby was a doughty performer here, while Paul Maas (whom one was accustomed to see very erect and bare-headed on a bicycle flying up St Giles') nervously jumped about in excitement. Rudolf Pfeiffer spoke quietly, when he could get a word in, and H. T. Wade-Gery with barely concealed satisfaction failed to impose sweet reason, mellifluously commended, on the discordant elements.

The Socratic Club, C. S. Lewis's own, so to speak, met often in a room in Magdalen on Saturdays and was distinguished for the scores of young women that sat upon the floor looking up to the Master for moral and other guidance. Sitting or lying on the floor seems to be a proper academic posture: it was said in Oxford then that D. Mackinnon, who showed commendable promise of eccentricity, started and ended his tutorials upright but was recumbent in between. But there were never enough chairs for the Socratic Society anyway.

As a Catholic I frequented the Newman Society which met in Cherwell Edge. There the relative increase in women members of the University due to the war was evident. Many of the members had an Irish background and a few of these I got to know well. Even then discussion in this kind of Catholic society was too little occupied with the dogmatic side of theology and too much with social problems and particularly with fertility control. It was evident that these were increasingly serious problems. As a graduate I was a member, indeed an officer for a time, of the Graduate Society, a struggling body artificially kept alive.

On the other hand playing rugby for Jesus was very lively. Twice a week we encountered some other College in competition for a Cup; but, although Jesus had one of the strongest teams in the competition, and might have been expected to be careful about winning, we all played a very open game resulting in much pleasure. I played wing three-quarter for the war-time University on a number of occasions. For me who, as a Jesuit scholastic, had been accustomed to play soccer desultorily, with half an eye on the Jesuit rule that forbade touching another, and fully dressed in old clothes, it was a relief to be unencumbered. The after-game firkin of beer consumed in somebody's rooms was also liberating and a convenient bucket made an urgent journey across a quadrangle, in the parlance of the times, unnecessary. Mixed hockey, walking on Sundays to keep rights-of-way open, and especially cycling – to Elsfield, Garsington, South Leigh, Burford, Blenheim or Wantage – raised one's spirits and kept one fit. And of course the Scholar-Gipsy country, Appleton and Bablock Hythe, had a very special appeal, which included the good ale at Appleton and a swim in the stripling Thames.

Less robust, but no less pleasing, distraction was provided by the Bach Choir conducted by the Choragus, Thomas Armstrong. Our major effort here was Beethoven's *Missa Solemnis*. But I got great pleasure out of J. S. Bach's *Komm, Jesu, Komm*, Parry's motets (dedicated to Hugh Allen and the choir itself) 'Lord, let me know mine end', and 'At the round earth's imagined corners', and some of John Dowland. In drama there were the entrancing presentations of Shakespeare against the backs of the medieval Benedictine buildings beside the lake in Worcester.

Truly Oxford is an enchanting city. The physical appearance of the Colleges alone can be enthralling. Dacre Balsdon has written of the pale January sun wheedling the warm ochre out of the fresh Oxford stone and turning the lichen on the tree trunks to strips of velvet. That was how I mostly saw her. But I remember even more the moon pouring down on the spires, pinnacles and battlements of the blacked-out city: there was no human light to dim the silver radiance on the Radcliffe Camera, the Codrington Library or St Mary's.

But there was a war on? Yes, indeed. On moonless nights the black-out left one bumping into people on the narrow footpaths of St Ebbe's. The seemingly never-ending convoys passing through Carfax and along the railway line; the tedious drone of aircraft towing gliders incessantly above; the sharp crash or hornet buzz of a fighter in the sky; the fearful spectacle of hundreds of bombers with their vapour trails carrying their deadly freight inevitably eastwards; and on D-day the unceasing procession of aircraft marked like wasps making southwards towards the coast; the crowds of servicemen and women of many nations and not unhappy-looking Italian prisoners clothed in brown; the diet of weak beer, ersatz coffee, beans, peanut butter, and especially dried egg, 'sawdust' sausages and spam – all these, the restricted life of the University itself and the wailing of the sirens at night reminded one that the war was ever present. Vacations spent at the British Museum in partly devastated London, and exposure to the unnerving 'doodle-bugs', bore in upon one the realization of how much Oxford was being spared. Then, an evidence of war, there was this great feeling of unity of purpose in the population as a whole.

I had my own internal conflicts. Although, as was usual with me, I was happy in my surroundings and occupation, I was unhappy particularly about the obligation, if I were to take on the priesthood, of commending to others doctrines I hardly clung to myself. It was all very well to receive assurance that difficulties of faith and other problems were common to all and difficult for all, and that one should, because of the transmission of authority through superiors, leave decision in such matters to them. This seemed the denial of personal responsibility. After Oxford I would normally proceed to a course in theology, where, since one would be brought face to face with dogma every day, trials were likely to become more intense. I had harrowing nights, wrote letters to a new and very matter-of-fact Provincial in Dublin, asking to leave the Society, and then followed up with telegrams withdrawing my request during the day. I do not wish to dwell on this agonizing trauma: it was intense, prolonged and shattering. In the end the Provincial and myself decided that I was not in a condition to start theology and he sent me to a small Jesuit community in Dublin in which some members were professors in University College. There I studied Palaeography with Ludwig Bieler and practised voice production in desperation almost daily on Dollymount Strand. But it was no use. In June 1945 the Provincial agreed with me that it was better that I leave the Society. I had received no Orders of any kind and so there were no problems. For years and years afterwards the crisis of my parting from something I deeply loved recurred urgently and frequently within my anxious dreams.

EPILOGUE

Soient Grecques, Egyptiennes,
De Hongrie ou d'autre pays,
Espaignolles ou Castellennes,
Il n'est bon bec que de Paris

– François Villon, 'Ballade des femmes de Paris'

I PASSED the summer of 1945 mostly at a lively hotel in Dalkey
to the south of Dublin. Looking down on that village from the
low hills above, one might at times, when the sun was high, be
excused for thinking that one was on a Greek island with white
villas descending to an azure sea. Farther south was the sweep
of Killiney Bay with here and there in the foreground an
unexpected palm or eucalyptus tree. But I also experienced the
bracing sea off the coast of Clare and the exotic scenery of
Kenmare, Parknasilla and Killarney. I had been trained to
expect that in such circumstances as those in which I now found
myself, I must surely need a rest. I rested very vigorously!

Among possibilities of career that seemed open to me was to
train my voice and become a professional singer. The idea had
occurred earlier to one or two senior Jesuit friends. What was
not really possible when I was a scholastic, might be possible
now. Thirty, however, seemed to me too advanced an age to
embark upon a career which in those days, in any case, might,
even if successful, provide a very uncertain livelihood. Moreover there was no sufficiently good training available in Dublin.
Vincent O'Brien, who had been an accompanist (and teacher?)
of John McCormack, was recommended to me. But I soon
discovered that he drifted very quickly from a narrow range of
exercises to practising such pieces as 'The Lark in the Clear Air'
and 'The Bard of Armagh'. He did help me through the tenor

role of the *Messiah*, which I found very satisfying, E. J. Moeran's setting of 'Seven Poems' of James Joyce (which is quite haunting), 'Die Mainacht' of Johannes Brahms, 'Vaghissima Sembianza' of Donaudy, and spoke of having a look at the Lieder of Hugo Wolf. He tended to come back, however, to Irish songs – 'My Lagan Love' and 'My Mary of the Curling Hair', of which he was inordinately fond. He was too old and perhaps I was not good enough. In any case I had in the meantime begun work in the department of Greek and Latin in University College, and the year's work I did with O'Brien did not get sufficient attention from either of us. Neither did I pursue discussions with Freddie Boland, then Secretary of the Department of External Affairs, later President of the United Nations (where he put down Khrushchev), about joining the diplomatic corps.

As it happened the department of Greek and Latin in University College was understaffed in relation to the great and increasing numbers of students who were obliged to take Latin. This subject was then imposed as a first-year subject on everyone who took Arts. At that time staff was recruited, where possible, from holders of the travelling studentship of the National University, which I had recently completed. Two years after my joining the staff, my former professor of Greek, Michael Tierney, by now unexpectedly President of the College, wrote in support of my candidature for the chair of Latin that he 'considered it a great stroke of good fortune for the College' to have secured my services in 1945. I wonder if he persisted in this view some ten to fifteen years later! Meanwhile I was grateful to him for his role in an appointment which quickly led to the professorship that I occupied until retirement.

After some less happy experiments I found myself lodged, very near University College, in the well-furnished house of Mrs Tyrrell, the owner of two nearby expensive Nursing

Homes. She was a wealthy woman who tolerated – at a price – a few men (only), who had a university connection (only), within her establishment. They were relegated to the top two floors and the use of a restaurant in the basement, while she dominated the scene in pink silk from her silken pink bedroom on the first floor. There she was enthroned beside the telephone, waited upon day and night by her personal nurse, the Matron of one of her Homes, complete with cap. Mrs Tyrrell observed our comings and goings and looked with expressed disfavour upon the introduction of any female visitors. As one passed through the hall, leaving the over-furnished reception rooms to the right, and mounted the stairs to the first floor and beyond, one feared that one would be summoned in a deep and slowly articulated masculine voice to the Presence. I was particularly open to this hazard since she knew that I was interested in singing, and was herself by way of being a patron of music (as of the Archbishop who visited very occasionally) and had her own plans for me in that connection. I thought her invitation to me to use her grand piano, whenever I wished, exceedingly generous until I discovered that whenever I played Matron was dispatched to report to me that just then Mrs Tyrrell had a headache.

Into this *mise en scène* a former colleague brought a French girl discreetly to tea one day in the summer of 1946. I had told him that I proposed to go to Paris to work on Eriugena at the Bibliothèque Nationale for the summer. I needed a visa and he thought that she, as secretary to the Ambassador, Comte Ostrorog, might be able to help me and, also, give me an introduction to someone in Paris. Would I invite them to tea? Matron, who by then had taken over several of my domestic chores and was always generously curious to be in on everything, got the tea laid on with fine china that was not mine. Thus I came to meet Odile, my future wife, when I opened to her the door of 8 Upper Pembroke Street. She carried an umbrella nearly as big as herself. She had a red jacket, a dark green tartan skirt, and over these I descried wavy brown hair, a gently tanned oval face and, above all, a pair of bright brown eyes.

> *She was a Phantom of delight*
> *When first she gleam'd upon my sight;*
> *A lovely apparition.*

Later I was to see in her many more of the qualities referred to in Wordsworth's inadequate poem.

Odile de Barthès de Montfort was born and grew up in Passy in the sixteenth *arrondissement* of Paris. I may, perhaps, be permitted to mention some *mildly* interesting coincidences at an earlier stage between the names of Barthès and O'Meara. Paul-Joseph Barthez, an ancestor of Odile, born at Montpelier in 1734, was professor of medicine and became famous for his theory of *vitalisme*, a theory showing the influence of Platonism. Later he was physician to Louis XVI and Marie-Antoinette and to Napoleon's father in 1785. He was nominated Physician to the Government, in effect to Napoleon, along with Corvisart in 1801, and was one of the first members inscribed on the roll of the Légion d'Honneur instituted by Napoleon in 1802. A better-known medical adviser and friend of Napoleon on St Helena, as the world knows (to echo Byron), was Barry O'Meara. Paul-Joseph Barthez had four younger brothers, the last of whom was born in 1755. As it happened, five O'Meara brothers, born in France over approximately the same period to John O'Meara, a captain in Clare's Irish Regiment, all officers of the Irish Brigade in the French service, attracted public attention at the same time. General Thomas O'Meara commanded Dunkirk in 1793 with 3000 men when the Duke of York with 35,000 demanded that he surrender the port as being 'destitute of any real defence'. O'Meara's reply is loved by the French:

Entrusted with the confidence of the French Republic, I have received your summons to surrender an important town. I desire to assure you that I shall defend it with the brave Republicans I have the honour to command.

The Duke immediately attacked, failed in his object, and suffered heavy losses. Another brother, William, as aide-de-camp to Marshal Lannes, was wounded beside him when Lannes was killed at the battle of Wagram in 1809. Both Thomas and William, having earlier suffered suspicion as 'aristos' – as so many refugee Irish were made – were also inscribed on the roll of the Légion d'Honneur within seven years of its institution – a detail which surprised Ambassador Badbedat when I was given the same honour a few years ago. The father of the five French O'Mearas came from Tipperary. One account of Barry O'Meara's birthplace gives it as Ballymona Cross near Nenagh. My own family is traced to Loughlin O'Meara of Slevoir towards the end of the seventeenth century. Slevoir is some twelve miles as the crow flies north-west from Nenagh. But there are plenty of O'Mearas in north Tipperary. I speak only of curious coincidences. Odile did in fact also have a relation with an Irish name – her grand-aunt ('tante') Yvonne, *née* O'Neill.

Platonism was not altogether absent from the period of our engagement. I had invited Père A.-J. Festugière OP to lecture in University College on the *Epinomis* of Plato. He had written some remarkable books, beginning with *Contemplation et vie contemplative selon Platon*, a translation of the *Corpus Hermeticum* and four volumes on *La révélation d'Hermès Trismégiste*. In addition he wrote a number of other both important and delightful works of which *Epicure et ses dieux* I find very *sympathique* indeed. He was one of the most intelligent men I ever met and wrote on many occasions in a beautifully poetic style. Yet with his small and spare stature he was gamin-like, even to advanced years, and looked and was mischievous, frequently wearing a broad grin. He came to Dublin for about a month before we were married and, having sampled two Dominican convents, quickly installed himself because of 'fever' in the Nursing Home beside me. There – apart from occasional sorties – he spent his days in his pyjamas sitting outside on his bed, smoking, and drinking Oxo, while he read through the proofs of my *Contra Academicos of St Augustine*, and laughingly – but seriously – indicated the many places where I might usefully insert his name in *Notes* and *Index*. His faith was of acute difficulty to him, and he often spoke of clinging on to it only by a thread. In blacker moods he was tempted to think that 'God had it in for him'. He felt despised and useless. He had been a young dandy, he said, during his studies at the Sorbonne, and when they were over neither he nor his father knew what he should do with himself. His father told him to join the Dominicans who in due course, he pretended, banished him to Jerusalem. When his book on the contemplative life according to Plato, written there, was a success, his Order brought him back to Paris where he duly got a job at the *École pratique des hautes études* and so launched himself on a brilliant academic career. During the month he was in Dublin he had frequent meals with us in the Unicorn, a restaurant much favoured by staff members of nearby University College. There he was hilarious company and composed many light verses on the quality of the food and the habits of the clientele. He prescribed for us the hotel for our honeymoon which should be spent at Talloires on the Lac d'Annecy. He would be there with us, of course. When he retreated to Paris I was conveyed from my lodgings in a Rolls-Royce ambulance three doors down to one of my landlady's Nursing Homes with a bad dose of exhaustion and food poisoning. My landlady knew how to do things! There I made a lifelong friendship with my doctor, Oliver FitzGerald, later professor of Therapeutics in University College. Odile and I were married in Newman's University Church in St Stephen's Green on July 24th 1947. Our honeymoon was spent during a memorable spell of warm sunny weather in Donegal, Achill and the Aran Isles. The Lac d'Annecy could not then have competed.

The senior member of Odile's family at the wedding, who had flown there in an aeroplane for the first time at eighty-one years of age, was a person of note. If Festugière represented the intellectualism of Plato, she represented the compassion of Christ. She had been married in 1893 to a wealthy but somewhat elderly syndic of the Paris Stock Exchange and thus was in a position to enjoy to the full *la grande époque*, the air of which she communicated to her dying day. During the First World War she ran a hospital at the front, and during the Second was among the ladies who felt that planting roses on the Maginot Line would be of great service to the *poilus*. For more serious services then, however, she was awarded the Croix de Guerre and became generally known as 'La Maréchale', 'car elle en avait le port et l'envergure' – as her collaborator and friend, Armand Marquiset, wrote of her. After the death of her first husband in 1918 she quickly parted from her money and in due course gave herself with characteristic verve and good humour to good works. One of these – 'Pour que l'Esprit Vive', an impossibly cheap restaurant for artists and students – she ran for the rest of her life along with Rita Essayan (Gulbenkian's sister), the aforementioned Armand and others. Odile had lived with la Maréchale in Paris during the war and until she came to Dublin.

And so Armand Marquiset entered our lives. Born in 1900 and brought up under the shadow of a sensitive father and a strong mother, he studied piano and composition with Nadia Boulanger. Tiring of the *vie mondaine* he decided to work for the destitute – the *clochards*. He gathered some 'brothers' about him and got some of them trained as cordon bleu cooks so as to supply worthy meals to the down-and-outs. His ideal was that of Mary, who took a pound of costly ointment of pure nard and anointed the feet of Jesus. What if Judas asked why the ointment was not sold and given to the poor! Hence on occasion Armand would present a diamond ring — importuned from some well-heeled friend — to a poor woman on an anniversary. Eventually the 'Little Brothers of the Poor' became a world-wide organization, and Armand had to find some new outlet for what he called his dream. India — and Mother Teresa — provided the beginnings of a new society, 'The Brothers to All Men'. Ireland was well placed to help here, since Irish personnel in India spoke English and, unlike the French, could get extended visas. Hence we were able to send, for example, young bankers and teachers, who were willing to take a few years off, to work at irrigation in Bihar. Armand himself, of course, distributed meals to the children and roses to the abandoned dying in some hospital wards in Calcutta. He was not happy, however, until he started another organization, called 'Brothers of Heaven and Earth', intended to meet any need of any one for at least a six-month period. It functioned from a shop in the middle of Paris above which was inscribed the legend 'Artisanat et Tendresse'. He consciously allowed himself to be exploited shamelessly in this endeavour — but that was his way. For him the great thing was sincerely to give respect, love, comfort and hope to the individual, no matter what his condition. He was a pious Catholic but opened his organizations to all in the service of all. He had a house in Co. Donegal where he stayed for long periods in the last eighteen years of his life. He died there in 1981 and was buried in the island cemetery of Cruit.

After a year or two Odile and I found a comfortable house of some character built around 1860 beside the very High Anglican St John's Church at the southern end of Sandymount. There between Sandymount Strand and Donnybrook, in an ecclesiastical enclave ringed by lofty trees, we lived in a type of house described by Maurice Craig in his *Classic Irish Houses of the Middle Size* as being almost unique to Dublin. Twenty granite steps led up to the ornate door where we substituted the name 'Montfort' for the former 'Inis Cealtra'. The drawing-room looked westwards over a rose-garden through the trees to the church tower and beyond it to the declining sun. Our three children, Dominique, Catriona and Odile, grew up in that pleasant house. Our life was shared with Tcheck, a cross between a poodle and a pekinese, who was devoted to each one of us for the whole of his long life, and a pekinese, Ku-Chi, who was too well bred to do more than accept our service with condescending hauteur. It was possible in those days even on a very modest salary to have indoor maids and a good gardener to look after greenhouse, vegetables, fruit and lawns on a few days a week. Dublin, a small capital city ringed by the mountains and the sea, was still beautiful, if a little down-at-heel, and sweet to live in with one's varied friends. One might try to do some useful work in helping to improve education at home, while participating fully in scholarly endeavour abroad. Life held plenty of promise.